Cycles
Possessing the Power of Living in Freedom

Brenda Murphy

Scripture quotations taken from the Amplified® Bible (AMPC), Copyright © 1954, 1958, 1962, 1964, 1965, 1987 by The Lockman Foundation, Used by permission. www.Lockman.org.

All verses marked LB are from The Holy Bible, Berean Literal Bible, BLB, Copyright ©2016 by Bible Hub, Used by Permission. All Rights Reserved Worldwide.

All verses marked BSB are from The Holy Bible, Berean Study Bible, BSB. Copyright ©2016, 2018 by Bible Hub, Used by Permission. All Rights Reserved Worldwide.

Scripture quotations marked CSB have been taken from the Christian Standard Bible®, Copyright © 2017 by Holman Bible Publishers. Used by permission. Christian Standard Bible® and CSB® are federally registered trademarks of Holman Bible Publishers.

Scriptures marked ESV are taken from the THE HOLY BIBLE, ENGLISH STANDARD VERSION (ESV): Scriptures taken from THE HOLY BIBLE, ENGLISH STANDARD VERSION ® Copyright© 2001 by Crossway, a publishing ministry of Good News Publishers. Used by permission.

Scriptures marked KJV are taken from the KING JAMES VERSION (KJV): KING JAMES VERSION, public domain.

Scripture quotations taken from the New American Standard Bible® (NASB), Copyright © 1960, 1962, 1963, 1968, 1971, 1972, 1973,1975, 1977, 1995 by The Lockman Foundation, Used by permission. www.Lockman.org.

Scriptures marked NIV are taken from the NEW INTERNATIONAL VERSION (NIV): Scripture taken from THE HOLY BIBLE, NEW INTERNATIONAL VERSION ®. Copyright© 1973, 1978, 1984, 2011 by Biblica, Inc.™. Used by permission of Zondervan.

Scriptures marked NKJV are taken from the NEW KING JAMES VERSION (NKJV): Scripture taken from the NEW KING JAMES VERSION®. Copyright© 1982 by Thomas Nelson, Inc. Used by permission. All rights reserved.

Scriptures marked NLT are taken from the HOLY BIBLE, NEW LIVING TRANSLATION (NLT): Scriptures taken from the HOLY BIBLE, NEW LIVING TRANSLATION, Copyright© 1996, 2004, 2007 by Tyndale House Foundation. Used by permission of Tyndale House Publishers, Inc., Carol Stream, Illinois 60188. All rights reserved. Used by permission.

Scriptures marked WEB are taken from the THE WORLD ENGLISH BIBLE (WEB): WORLD ENGLISH BIBLE, public domain.

Copyright © 2019 Brenda Murphy

All rights reserved. No part of this book may be reproduced in any form or by any electronic or mechanical means, including information storage and retrieval systems, without permission in writing from the publisher, except by reviewers, who may quote brief passages in a review, or as allowed by the Fair Use Act.

ISBN-10: 1-7325363-9-2
ISBN-13: 978-1-7325363-9-5

Cover design by Rick Schroeppel – 2020 Book Cover Design

Publisher: bylisabell
Radical Women
(DBA)
PO Box 782
Granbury, TX
76048
www.bylisabell.com

This book is written and dedicated to those individuals who have lived their lives in silent pain and under the umbrella and scope of judgment, mistreatment and in some cases physical, emotional or mental abandonment.

Perhaps you, yourself may have always believed nothing would ever change for your life. You bought into the enemies lies that you would always be bound and chained to the things and situations that kept you ashamed, downtrodden or embarrassed.

Today, as you read Cycles, I decree and declare that the spirit of God is going to transform your life through the reading of His Word forever!

~Brenda Murphy~

"The people walking in darkness have seen a great light on those living in the land of deep darkness, a light has dawned."

Isaiah 9:2, NIV

Table of Contents

Part One 1
- Introduction of a Cycle 2
- Why Does the Hamster Need a Wheel? 8
- Seeing Double 22
- The Voice of Condemnation 34

Part Two 41
- Been There, Done That 42
- Right Back Where I Started 49
- Haven't I Been Here Before? 55
- This Time has to be Different 61

Part Three 69
- Why Does This Keep Happening to Me? 70
- The Devil Made Me Do It 75
- I'll Start Tomorrow 91
- It's No Big Deal 99

Part Four 102
- What's Keeping You From Breaking the Cycle? 103
- Lay Aside Every Excuse 122
- The Moment You Realize That God Is Bigger Than Your Mess, Everything Changes For You 127

Part Five 134
- From a Different Angle 135
- Broken Chains & Released Vision 139

Surrendered Will 150

Gracious Grace 158

Conclusion – The Leading of the Good Shepherd 163

Personal Evaluation 172

References 176

About the Author 177

Acknowledgement

This book is to acknowledge all the beautiful, incredible, resilient and positive individuals who stood with me at times in my earlier years when I was still unfolding in my life's baby steps, trying desperately to lay hold of my godly footage.

Cycles is dedicated to those who loved me into change, hope, peace of mind and confidence so that one day, I could walk and even sprint, if need be, into my destiny.

Thank you to the beautiful souls who co-labored with me. Prayed for me. Cried with me and in some instances, placed compassionate arms around me and shouldered me in my growth.

Today, through your multiple prayers and generous compassion, I live my life daily in a true sense of purpose and resolve. Thank you for pouring into my life continually.

Sincerely,
Brenda

Part One

Introduction of a Cycle

Good morning, class. Today's subject matter centers on the word "Cycle." Raise your hand if any of you are familiar with these situations or statements.

❖ You asked, or someone you know asked you, to borrow money promising to pay it back when you got some cash. However, two, three, four or even five years later, the funds have never been returned. Still, you or they continued the act of loaning anyway, and one or both of you are upset because none of those promises worked out.

❖ You can easily dish out high dosages of criticism, but you cannot handle when someone is brutally honest with you. Your behavior is justified to you at least in your own eyes, whether you're right or wrong. After all, that's just the way you are. You've always spoken your mind.

❖ "I speak my mind regardless of who it may offend because of what I've been through."

❖ "I will not allow anyone else to hurt or disrespect me ever again."

❖ "It's okay because someone did it to me. I felt justified in doing it to someone else."

❖ "What does it matter to them, they're rich and don't need it anyway. Heck, they probably won't even miss it."

❖ "It's okay. It's alright. He/she didn't mean to hit me — I should not have kept pressuring him/her and asking too many questions. He/she says it's the first and last time something like this is going to happen. He/she apologized and acts ashamed for hitting me."

❖ "Okay, okay, so there are rumors he/she is cheating on me going on around town. But at least he/she comes home to me eventually at night. Other people should mind their business."

❖ "He's not a womanizer. He only lashes out when provoked and feels backed into a corner. After all, no one likes to be placed under a magnifying glass."

❖ "Okay, okay God, I know I asked you to please get me out of debt three years ago, and You did. But I promise — if you bring me out one more time, I will never do this again."

❖ "I realize he/she is not the marrying type, but at least having someone in my life is better than being alone. I mean no one's perfect, right?"

❖ "I am thankful for the job I have, but they expect too much out of me. I mean, they cannot expect me to show up every day. God, I need something more."

❖ "That's it. I am leaving this church because the people are not friendly. They're fake. They say one thing but then do another. I am going to find me another church home across town where the people are much friendlier—perhaps a smaller church where everyone knows each other."

❖ How about this one. "You're nothing. Your momma and daddy were nothing, and you are only a carbon copy of them. I don't even know why you feel the need to keep trying so hard."

❖ "Now look at you. You think you have arrived because you live in this fancy house and drive this expensive car. You think that makes you somebody? Well, don't forget where you came from. Remember, I know all about you and your past."

Oh, I see quite a few hands raised during our little question segment. So that tells me at least each of us in this room can identify with at least one, two or several of these statements.

Thank you for your honesty today. There is absolutely nothing to feel guilty about or ashamed of because each one of us played one of these roles—played a part in one of these scenes. Maybe you had a starring or recurring act as the headliner in most of these characters in life, and the only way to recognize the play is by reading the script.

Would you like to know what that play is called? What's that? You would? Well, lean in closer. Here it comes. It's called "Cycles."

You see, a cycle is nothing more than repeated offenses without any thought of change or the ability to move forward and out of it on your own.

Cycles are the vicious circle that keeps us preoccupied, burdened, taxed, bounded, overwhelmed, needy, guilt-ridden, apologetic, and desperate. Often, we remain pitiful and saddened over things we should have dealt with, thrown out or released a very long time ago.

Cycles keep you and I up at night when we should be in bed getting a good night's sleep. They make us apologize countless times for things we think we're guilty of but do not have any concrete truth or proof to say otherwise. And many times, our apology is for things we didn't even do, cause or start.

Cycles cause us to forfeit what is rightfully ours whether we earned those things, inherited them or received them as gifts.

Cycles cause us to give up our respect, dignity, and integrity, forfeit our boundaries, let down our guards, bend over backward, temporarily lose our minds and cheapen our self-esteem to please or appease someone else or temporarily make them "happy" at our expense.

And cycles cause us to shut down, sit down, lay down and sleep around all in the name of pretending to be something or someone we are not so others can remain comfortable and protected from their fragile and aloof ego.

Until this spirit is confronted, the robber is still allowed to roam free on the streets of our hearts and minds, continuing to sabotage and highjack our joy, peace and liberty at a fraction of the cost of living.

Because we don't confront this spirit, we provide for these robbers the liberty to live a reckless lifestyle far beyond what they deserve. And in the process, we give them the ability to entitlements they never earned.

Cycle means not being strong enough to confront the issues and situations that dogged us, hunted us down like an animal, or berated us. If not all of our life, it has been the majority of it. And we have not had the confidence to oppose or deal with the issues that keep us in cycles.

Having the courage or the fortitude to walk out, get out, or fall out of what has held you down, put you down, pushed you down or even ran you down and left you for dead for entirely too long.

Cycles are when you allow yourself to become so accustomed to the nonsense, vulgarity, disappointments, discouragement, disheartenment and disillusions for so long you started believing the lie yourself.

Cycles are vicious, never-ending loopholes because they are distorted, misguided lies straight from the very pit of hell, designed to take away the liberty, promises, blessings and fulfillment God promised you and me.

Think about this for just a moment. If anyone in your life has to stoop so low as to use language, words, motives, lies, distortion or pure evil to control you or to discredit your good name just so they can pretend to be something they are not, he or she must be an extremely low-minded person. And a low-minded person is considered sordid, improper, bad, wrong, evil, wicked, iniquitous, sinful, unscrupulous, unseemly and unsavory with a shady character and disposition.

The ability to continue a relationship with a mindset of someone or something that wants to keep you connected to a dysfunctional cycle is like willingly agreeing to run on a treadmill like a hamster in the polar opposite direction of where you are trying to go.

What does this behavior look like? It's like looking into the mirror at home, wondering if they look like you. Cycles in your life will never be broken as long as you are willing to be a cycle at the hands of those who are more than willing to use, abuse, and trample over you.

Why Does the Hamster Need a Wheel?

When I think of cycles, I think of the act or actions of a repeat offender—constant, no change, continuous and little improvement with the same or similar outcomes.

Simply put, the life of a repeat offender is not that they are necessarily horrific people or people without souls, heart or meaning—they don't understand yet who they really are in Christ Jesus. Therefore, they continue the rat race of living in a vicious low-mentality lifestyle.

Such an existence reminds me of the lifestyle of a hamster, which in my opinion can be somewhat related to the activities of humankind. Always on the go with a million and one things left to accomplish. Unfortunately, they don't get very far. On a wheel of negative thoughts, broken dreams, doubts, and fears, on many occasions, humans carry bottomed out self-esteem images of themselves in their self-preserved mirrors. There they overly concern themselves with issues they allow others to paint of them.

To further compound the problem, many people intentionally, or perhaps unintentionally, load themselves up with mega tasks and projects that quite frankly cannot be done within the superficial timeframe allotted.

In the process, they never stop to honestly count the cost of whether they have the time, energy, finances, skillset, talents, resources, manpower, ability or necessary help to accomplish all of that in a lifetime. In most cases, they don't notice the lack of resources to get off the wheel and live, but like a hamster, continually run in circles, doing much at a significant personal cost.

An individual who allows themselves to get wrapped up in someone else's cycle is one who permits themselves to be controlled by the kneejerk reaction of others. These individuals have the ability to meet everyone else's needs according to the other person's timetable, no matter what the "emergency" costs them personally.

People who pull others into their cycles do not care whether you can meet your monthly debt obligation. Instead, they insist, "Let me borrow this or that until…" Yeah, you guessed it right. That date or time never comes.

A cycle is a con-artist mentality person draped in a masquerade outfit, declaring to be something they are not. Always waiting for the next victim they can lash themselves to, they then bleed them dry. When the mission has been accomplished, they move on slowly to the next target.

Heaven help the one not paying attention to the flow of an opportunist waiting for a chance to usurp their authority on the kindness of others through the disguise of being a "blessing to them."

Years ago, when I had my first Women's Conference, I learned about such a one. This woman, through a church I frequented, asked if I had someone to do the videography. When I admitted I didn't, she offered to do it for free. She refused even when I insisted on paying her because that moment was extremely special to me.

Not only did she botch the job, she acted completely unprofessional. The woman held the original footage of my videotape and refused to give it to me.

She suddenly remembered but forgot to tell me before the taping. "I never give the original tapings to anyone because I like to keep them for myself."

To make matters worse, this individual acted unprofessionally, and her demeanor turned extremely ungodly, especially when she added, "Because of the number of requests for videotapes, I will now have to charge you $25.00 per tape to cover my time in making copies for you."

Doing business with or entering into any agreement with an individual of this type of mindset is dangerous on so many levels. Such a person lacks moral character and honest disposition.

This thought brings me to the subject matter of how a hamster must feel. If the animal were able to communicate to his abductor who sees him as nothing more than a pet held in a cage, what might he think?

Imagine if you will the cycle life of a hamster. From day one, God never created him to be held up in a cage of any size. Meanwhile, the innocent being runs around in circles for the sheer enjoyment of those who delight themselves in standing around, staring at the hamster's confusion.

For the record, it is said that lots of hamsters are desert animals, some coming from Syria, others originating from areas such as Northern China. They inhabit desert or sparse rocky spaces, both of which are places with extreme variations in temperature, ranging from scorching hot to extremely cold in a short span of time. In some regions, these fluctuations are one of the reasons hamsters burrow underground and have quite a dense fur. These wild characteristics are particularly noticeable in hamster species not bred in captivity for very long, such as the Roborovski.

As well as fluctuations in temperature, wild hamsters have to deal with a high degree of variation in volumes of food they can find. They evolved to deal with this by gathering an elevated amount when available and storing it for use in times of less abundance. To help with this potentially life-saving task, over a long period their bodies evolved to store a great deal of food in two flaps of skin — the areas of their mouths known as the 'cheek pouches.' These handy pouches are capable of storing large amounts of food, so the hamster can carry a lot of tasty snacks back to their nest or stash them away, saving for later.

Another adaptation wild hamsters developed is their coloring. While Syrian hamsters have been in captivity a long time, their wild counterparts and other pet hamster species still retain the markings and colors of their native forms.

Wild hamsters often have light brown or grey-colored backs and pale stomachs. Their colored backs help them blend into the surrounding scenery to make it harder for predators to spot them, while their lightly-colored bellies reflect extreme temperatures from the sand or rock they scurry around on all night.

While purchasing a hamster as a cute little pet for home usage or fun, the new owner should consider several things prior to taking this type of animal from its original habitat:

- Feeding a hamster
- Hamster's Health
- Hamster's Health Care
- Hamster's Housing
- Hamster's Hygiene
- Hamster's Illnesses
- Hamster's Toys
- Hamster's Care

Now, at the outset, essential things of this nature may or may not have even occurred to the owner who at the time of purchase only foresees the hamster as a "pet" for pleasure. He or she may not consider the discomfort of the hamster itself.

Hamster wheels allow the animals to run even though they don't have a lot of room in their cages. In the wild, a hamster can run for several miles in a single night, but they obviously can't do this when confined to a cage. At least, not without a wheel.

With a wheel, your hamster can run surprisingly long distances without ever having to leave home. In fact, hamsters running in wheels have been known to run more than five miles in a single night!

Unfortunately, the hamster doesn't realize they are merely running in circles over and over again, accomplishing very little. At the end of the day, this is not considered as progress but instead trained behavior wrapped up in a well-behaved cycle.

All this running is excellent exercise for your hamster, which means they're more likely to stay fit and healthy and not get too fat! However, the end goal for the hamster is freedom to roam about as it was designed in the first place before capture and someone's "great idea" to keep them in captivity by mankind.

It's also thought hamsters enjoy running as it goes some way toward replacing exploring, which they do in the wild but can't when cooped up in a cage in the privacy of someone's home.

I can understand to some degree why the hamster trapped in his/her cage and held hostage cannot get out. The wheel helps keep them fit by running in cycles, but that's all it accomplishes day in and day out.

Why do we, as human beings, allow ourselves to continue in cycles just for the sake of being busy, looking important, or maybe pleasing others? How's that working for you?

For the hamster, as long as they remain cooped up in the cage, they are limited, trapped and bound. Some might even declare the animals are stuck or ensnared because the hamsters are not free to be what they were originally created to be and to do.

In a lot of ways, I would say hamsters are not the only ones who foster this type of behavior. The one exception is the hamster doesn't have a choice. They are being held captive by their owner and kept against their will. We, on the other hand, have been freed by the Blood of the Lamb. If we stay in cycles, perhaps it is only out of a sense of fear, dread, obligation or tolerance.

Some individuals live their lives in the same or similar fashion as the poor hamster, forever running but never making any plausible progress. They complain they are weary and worn, perhaps even wounded, but they continue to volunteer for more.

I use to have a co-worker. Regardless of the subject, she was the queen of all subject matters, in every engaging topic.

Take the Christmas holiday. She declared, "Oh my goodness, I have entirely too much to do. I have to travel out of town for work four days out of five before the holiday. And when I return, I have to cook dinner for 27 guests plus bake pies."

When asked if she requested any of her guests to bring a covered dish to take some of the load off her, you would think I cursed out her mother.

With a snarled look on her southern face and wad of curly hair on top of her head, she leaned back and said, "Absolutely not! Those are my guests, and that's my responsibility."

She reminded me of Blanche from the Golden Girls.

Anyway, studies found that hamsters with running wheels gnaw on their cages less if they live in the right type of enclosure. And according to the reports, female hamsters with running wheels give birth to more pups per litter than those without wheels!

While I am not saying or calling any human being a hamster, I am using the metaphor to demonstrate some of the behavioral tendencies of mankind compared to the activity of the caged animal. When we do not take time out, preferably before we start our day, to sit in a quiet place before the Lord and ask Him to order our steps, we can end up being totally out of alignment with the plan God had for us to accomplish that day. Therefore, it ends up being a day of unfulfillment both naturally and spiritually.

The more we allow ourselves to be controlled and governed by the "emergencies" of others (caused by their lack of planning, praying and seeking God for themselves), the more additional bondage we allow heaped upon us. And that comes at the expense of personal health, joy and peace of mind.

Another fascinating thing about hamster activity is that there are specific kinds of hamster wheels. Not only required for a hamster to be productive at what they do, but they are also necessary and available. In the hamster's world, there are both metal and plastic hamster wheels available. Each type has pros and cons. Metal wheels tend to last longer than plastic ones. Metal is a stronger material than plastic, so hamsters are much less likely to damage "metal wheels" by chewing on them.

In this instance, I believe the hamster's distorted

mindset makes him think he plays it safe. In reality, he creates something that causes him more confinement. He remains enclosed rather than looking for a way out of his entrapment to roam free.

So it is with humanity. Sometimes, even when God desires to show us a way out of what entraps us, we keep seeking more conveniences. Unbeknownst to us, they often keep us bound and entangled by the things that hinder our progress.

Unfortunately, metal wheels are usually made with rungs rather than one solid piece. Hamster legs are quite fragile and can easily get injured if they fall through the gaps between rungs while running. Thus, this is often not the obvious choice for hamster lovers to purchase. If they deem plastic a safer option for protecting the hamster, owners don't mind paying extra costs to replace wheels frequently.

When a person continues to foster the behavior traits of a hamster, if not careful, the lies of the enemies work the same way. He keeps you and me forever on the destructive cycle in the same manner of life. And trust me, he isn't a thoughtful owner who cares if the rungs catch us and destroy our legs.

The enemy causes our thinking to become distorted. He convinces us if we keep doing the same ole' thing long enough and work at it hard enough, we will eventually get the desired results. In the process, he entices us to stay isolated, closed off or under the scope of a disguise that everything is going to be okay without a single change. (Incidentally, some call that insanity.)

The plastic wheels in a cage for hamsters are often made from one solid piece of plastic rather than rungs, which is safer for the hamster with no gaps for their legs to fall through. The design continuously allows the hamster to stay encaged while continually running around in the same cycle.

Sound familiar?

Hamster lovers might ask the retailer about the appropriate wheel size. Experts recommend a minimum wheel size of 6.5 inches for dwarf hamsters. Roborovski and larger, including Syrian hamsters need at least eight inches. The wheel size doesn't matter much, though. They all train to the size of their cages because the hamster realizes he has to make the necessary adjustments to the space provided.

Interestingly, the larger a wheel is the less a hamster has to arch its back providing a more similar experience to running on the flat ground in the wild. In other words, the larger cage gives the hamster the false impression of freedom, although he is far from it.

So it is with cycles. Until we are willing to acknowledge our entrapment or bondage, even if it is our personal unwillingness to be set free and move out in courage and faith, choosing to believe God for what He alone promised, we remain stuck. We continue to read our Bibles, pray and even fast but never step out in what the Word of God says we can lay hold to.

Instead, we become complacent, lackadaisical, fearful, and even discouraged enough to keep looking out from our traps and seeing the blessing over there.

Rather than taking the keys, unlocking the cages of our various bondages and coming out, we stay on our wheel. All while the Word of God has already declared we are free to go. *"A slave is not a permanent member of the family, but a son belongs to it forever. So if the Son sets you free, you will be free indeed."* (John 8:35-36, BSB)

Look at it this way—even when the owner of a hamster sees its pet in an uncomfortable space never designed for him, instead of setting the animal free into the wild for which it was created, he or she chooses to purchase a bigger place of confinement. There, the creature remains in total bondage for the person's pleasure and enjoyment.

The owner of a hamster hears, "Should you ever see your hamster running with an arched back in his confined cage, it is horrible for a hamster's health. If you ever see your pets arching their backs while running, then you should buy a larger wheel for them as soon as possible."

Wow. Did it ever occur to the owner that the hamster was never created to be a "pet" full of discomfort and the inability to live life in the wild as a free agent and as intended?

We must not become wise in our own eyes but instead always seek God for His plan in our lives. Then we won't allow ourselves to be caught up in busyness, overwhelmed by the sheer mundane frame-ups of this world. When that happens, we don't notice it leading us away from what God originally purposed for our lives.

In the same way, a hamster wheel sounds noisy, so

it is with the lifestyle of mankind running around without purpose. We make a lot of noise but no beneficial progress. Yes, we may have started several projects and completed a few to their outcomes. But take note of what this lifestyle may have caused with your health, relationships or personal time spent in the presence of God.

Make no mistake, making a lot of unproductive noise, much like the squeak of hamster wheels, can be counter-productive at the same time. In other words, all that running in cycles is basically, a waste of time.

Another important note about hamsters. Remember, hamsters are often active at night. If your hamster wheel squeaks, then you'll probably get disturbed by your hamster's running. Inevitably, he'll want to run when you want to sleep!

In comparison, another determent about a cycle brings to mind a saying. "There is no rest for the weary." In that constant state of running, when you lie down for sleep at night, you assume the restful position, but the activity of your mind (the cycle) continues running at high rates of speed, trying to accomplish something you have no control over. While the body may sleep, it never enters total rest because the mind can't stop running.

Although it may be tempting to avoid putting a wheel in your hamster cage or remove it if it gets too loud, this is definitely not a good idea. As we already explained, a hamster wheel is an essential part of your hamster's physical and psychological health. If the animal must remain in a state of bondage, at least give it the change to stay fit.

Can I tell you the only real reason the enemy desires to keep the people of God fit? He wants to continue using those not in tune or paying attention to the vicious cycle they have been in for most of their lives. Rather than take personal ownership of exhaustion, frustration or unhappiness, they pass their state on to others who had nothing to do with their depleted joy.

In order to get off this unintended treadmill of life, we must be careful to think about where we place the hamster cage in our lives intentionally or unintentionally.

We should not be content to place our over-taxed plans, agendas, projects and meetings in other places on our "to do lists" or daily journals. We must keep them far away from our peace, joy and rest in the Lord.

Finally, if you can still hear your hamster's cycle wheel spinning, try adding a bit of the Word of God's promises where the wheel of stress meets the spindle of doubt, and believe God for deliverance. This should lubricate and dismantle the lies and schemes of the wheels of deception from the enemy and reduce the squeaking and rattling of his untruth.

To replace the hamster wheel of the vicious cycle you have been on for a while in your life, let me recommend the following replacement steps.

1. Trust in the Lord with All Your Heart
2. Don't Depend on You.
3. Cry out to God.
4. Run from Evil.

5. Put God First in Your Life.
6. Check Yourself by God's Word.

Don't forget—you must choose a wheel suitable for your hamster's cycle size! Well, that sounds like a job for God alone. After all, He is the only One I know who is more than able, capable, reliable, dependable and faithful to see us through it all.

I don't know about you, but I am not asking Him simply to "break every chain." I am asking Him to obliterate them and banish them from my walk in Him forever!

Seeing Double

Have you ever seen a family where the father has a problem with uncontrollable anger, alcohol, or abuse? Perhaps his son seems to have been 'handed it,' and the grandpa had the same problem.

Or have you noticed that not only do you suffer from something such as persistent, irrational fears or depression, but your mother and her father suffered from it as well? Many people today live under bondage the sins of their forefathers brought them under.

Have you ever met someone with the mindset of worrying all the time? Perhaps you have that attitude. Whether a problem exists or not, you merely worry, stress, and doubt in advance. You know, in case something comes up in the future to worry about, you'll be ahead of the game. Perhaps you are the type of person who can pray away a storm cloud but turn in a few minutes and bring down the rain by your words of doubt and saying the polar opposite of what you prayed.

Have you ever sincerely thought you dealt with something to the point of getting rid of it? Then that same issue, concern, problem or situation rears its ugly head again.

Did you perhaps grow up with or around someone who never could seem to find words to encourage you but had no qualms or shortage of criticism about every single thing you tried to do to the best of your ability?

Then he or she wondered why you struggled with low self-esteem.

> *Keeping mercy for thousands, forgiving iniquity and transgression and sin, and that will by no means clear the guilty; visiting* (punishing) *the iniquity of the fathers upon the children, and upon the children's children, unto the third and to the fourth generation.*
> Exodus 34:7, KJV
> (parentheses mine)

> *Our fathers have sinned, and are not; and we have borne* (been punished for) *their iniquities.*
> Lamentations 5:7, KJV
> (parentheses mine)

Beyond learned behavior, many children tend to be messy if their parents are messy. Spiritual bondage is passed down from one generation to another. Some symptoms of a generational curse are continual negative patterns of something being handed down from generation to generation.

Often adopted people end up with the same characteristics as their birth parents. Not because they were around their birth parents to learn how they behaved, but because they inherited their spiritual bondage.

Another common symptom of generational curses is family illnesses that seem to just walk from one person down to the next. (Cancer is a common physical manifestation of spiritual bondage.) Continual financial difficulties (they continually hit roadblocks in their finances), mental problems, persistent, irrational fears, and depression also flow between generations.

Anything that seems to be a persistent struggle or problem handed down from one generation to another may very well be a generational curse.

There are multiple reasons and purposes of a generational curse. To some degree, I think the punishment of future generations concerning the sins of their fathers could have been because of God's bitter hatred for sin.

He required somebody who practiced witchcraft to be put to death (Exodus 22:18). He knows that one of the most prized possessions you have is your children, and therefore, it makes sin a lot harder to commit when you realize you are not the only one punished for it. Your children are going to pay the price for your foolishness also.

That's what I believe is the reason behind generational curses. The whole human race fell thanks to Adam's sin, for that matter. Thankfully, we know the price for generational curses has been paid!

The good news is that once you accept Jesus, the transference of bondage stops from your ancestors by means of generational curses. You can no longer receive spiritual bondage in this manner from your parents once you accept Jesus.

Christ was made a curse so we can be freed from the curses that sin (both ours and those of our forefathers) brought us. "*Christ hath redeemed us from the curse of the law, being made a curse for us: for it is written, Cursed is every one that hangeth on a tree:"* (Galatians 3:13, KJV)

Once you become a child of God, no longer will the sins of your forefathers cause curses to transfer into your life. *"In those days they shall say no more, The fathers have eaten a sour grape, and the children's teeth are set on edge. But every one shall die for his own iniquity: every man that eateth the sour grape, his teeth shall be set on edge."* (Jeremiah 31:29-30, KJV)

So why do so many believers seem to be living under a generational curse? This puzzled me before I understood how it works too. What may need to be dealt with, though, is any bondage already passed down to you before you came into covenant with God.

The legal grounds are certainly paid for on the cross and therefore broken. The only thing left to do is cast out any spirits (wrong beliefs, doubts and fears) that gained entrance before you accepted Jesus.

Non-believers remain affected even after Jeremiah 31:29-30 makes it clear believers are redeemed from generational curses. The next chapter in Jeremiah (32:18, KJV)) clearly says, *"Thou shewest lovingkindness unto thousands, and recompensest the iniquity of the fathers into the bosom of their children after them: the Great, the Mighty God, the LORD of hosts, is his name."* Apparently, generational curses are still in effect, but for who is the big question.

Ezekiel 18:2-3 (KJV) tells us, *"What mean ye, that ye use this proverb concerning the land of Israel, saying, the fathers have eaten sour grapes, and the children's teeth are set on edge? As I live, saith the Lord GOD, ye shall not have occasion any more to use this proverb in Israel."* (Note the keywords "in Israel." The verse refers to those in covenant with God, which means us as believers, not the rest of the world.)

Obviously, generational curses are alive and well in the lives of those who live outside the new covenant with God (non-believers). Understanding possible triggers that can affect a generational curse today, we need to go a little deeper.

It is possible for demons to enter a child before he accepts Jesus, then remain dormant or hidden in that child's life until sometime later in his or her life when it manifests (or makes itself known).

Sometimes, when a person heads for the ministry, it seems like the devil kicks up his ugly heels and causes havoc for that person. Other times, a line of fear runs in the family tree but isn't manifested in a person's life until they get themselves involved in something fearful, such as watching a demonic movie. All of a sudden, the spirits in that person's life "come alive" so to speak, and make themselves known through fear of being in the dark, being alone or lashing out when they feel backed into a corner. They were there all along, but unexpectedly, they come out into the open.

The solution is to cast them out.

If you involved yourself in any sin or opened any doors in your own life while 'awaking' or triggering the spirits, then it's important that you clear up any legal grounds (or strongholds) you gave the enemy in your life relating to the bondage.

For example, if you went to see a demonic movie,

and it seemed to have triggered spirits of fear in your life handed down to you, then it's important to repent for going to see such a movie before trying to cast out any spirits.

It's also possible you picked up the spirits from such a movie without them even being there in the first place and added to spirits already inside you. It's always a good idea to clear up any legal grounds or strongholds in your own life before casting spirits out.

I believe unforgiveness is a great way to 'trigger' generational spirits, so I would be on the lookout for any bitterness or unforgiveness in your heart as well. A common sight is when a spirit of cancer runs down the family tree. Bitterness is a great way to trigger those spirits.

Unforgiveness is a serious sin that blocks forgiveness of your sins as well (Matthew 6:15), which creates ample legal grounds for the enemy in your life. Unforgiveness in itself puts us into the enemy's hands (Matthew 18:23-35), say nothing about awaking any evil spirits in us already!

Sometimes, even though the curse may be canceled, the demons remain. Just as other demons don't automatically leave at the time of salvation, neither do the demons you get from your ancestors automatically depart either.

Let's say you accept Jesus at age 15. Because you were born a sinner and outside of God's covenant, you still lived under the curses handed down to you. And demons can enter through those curses.

Once you accepted Jesus, those curses are broken automatically, but often the demons that entered in before you accepted Jesus still need to be cast out or renounced in and over your life.

In other words, the curse is already broken, and there's no need for you to break any generational curses. But the demons who entered into you through those curses before you accepted Jesus may still need to be cast out. That's why it seems so many believers are living under generational curses when the Bible makes it clear we have been freed from any curses handed down from our forefathers!

Down through the years, my parents experienced good health well into their 60's, while it seems the family tree held many health problems handed down from our ancestors. Still, my parents seemed almost immune to the health problems in the family tree. Sure, they took care of their bodies for the most part, but they also believed they lived in freedom from the curses handed down in the family tree.

They were freed from the effects by merely standing on what Jesus did for them on the cross!

There's a neat story in Mark 9:17-27, where Jesus deals with what is almost certainly a generational curse (verse 21). Notice Jesus didn't have the boy confess the sins or iniquities of his ancestors, but He cast out the demons that entered in through the curse.

That's how I believe we are to deal with the effects of a generational curse. Since the curse has been broken, all we have left to do is cast the demons out that entered into a person's life back before he or she became a Christian (before the curse was broken).

In the process, Christians must learn to confess what is rightfully ours! We know our generational curses have been broken in Jesus' name, but I still like to confess verbally what is going on and what is rightfully ours anyway. Because there's power in our verbal confessions, speaking out loud helps us realize we are set free. It also lets the enemy know he's in trouble.

Here's a great sample confession prayer you can use to do just that.

> *In the name of Jesus, I confess the sins and iniquities of my parents (name specific sins if known), grandparents (name specific sins if known), and all other ancestors. I declare that by the blood of Jesus, these sins have been forgiven and Satan and his demons can no longer use these sins as legal grounds in my life!*
>
> *In the name of Jesus, and by the power of His blood, I now declare that all generational curses have been renounced, broken and severed, and I am no longer under their bondage!*
>
> *In the name of Jesus, I declare myself and my future generations loosed from any bondages passed down to me from my ancestors. AMEN!*

Let's consider another factor. Other things seem like generational curses but aren't. Perhaps the most common is if there an ungodly soul tie formed between you and one of your ancestors. That tie can also allow for the transferring of spirits. There is more to learn on this subject in the teaching on *Soul Ties*.

Ignorance: Another source of bondage that can keep you in cycles is what I also believe some people can live under that seems like a generational curse, simply because they believe it's still in effect.

We need to know it is NO LONGER in effect, and we have been **FREED** from any generational curses we used to live under. Jesus makes it very clear we can be held in bondage to sin through ignorance (John 8:31-36), and I believe the same is true with bondage to generational curses.

> *To the Jews who had believed him, Jesus said, "If you hold to my teaching, you are really my disciples. Then you will know the truth, and the truth will set you free." They answered him, "We are Abraham's descendants and have never been slaves of anyone.*
> *How can you say that we shall be set free?" Jesus replied, "Very truly I tell you, everyone who sins is a slave to sin. Now a slave has no permanent place in the family, but a son belongs to it forever. So if the Son sets you free, you will be free indeed."*
> John 8:31-36, NIV

To explain in a nutshell, I don't believe Christians can live under generational curses. But I do believe spirits (old habits, mindsets, lack of understanding and rituals) that entered through those curses before they accepted Jesus sometimes affect them.

In the same way, many people's actions before they

came to Christ landed them in demonic bondage and caused them to pick up demons and sometimes, demonic ways and mannerisms. Those demons are not automatically shed at the time of salvation, so they often need to be cast out. The same is true with demons that enter in through generational curses (a doorway to demons).

With people who still trust in tariff card readings, palm readings, horoscopes and the like, I believe these spirits entered through a generational curse of belief.

"*And these signs shall follow them that believe; in my name shall they cast out devils...*" (Mark 16:17, KJV). Learn of the ***Spiritual Authority*** Jesus has given you over demon spirits, and by faith, you can command those spirits to leave you in Jesus' name!

If you can't seem to get them out, try prayer and fasting. As Jesus clearly stated, some demons won't come out unless you have a higher level of faith that only prayer and fasting can bring you (Matthew 17:19-21).

Lastly, there is also another type of generational curse. The type of curses handed down as a result of an ancestor's sin is automatically atoned for on the cross, providing we don't hide the sins of our forefathers in our hearts. Holding sin in our hearts is never a good idea — whether it's ours of the sins of our ancestors.

But there's another kind of generational curse handed down, and it's a spoken curse that takes a toll on future generations as well. We see this kind of curse in action in Genesis 9:24-25 (KJV). "*And Noah awoke from his wine and knew what his younger son had done unto him. And he said, Cursed be Canaan; a servant of servants shall he be unto his brethren."*

As the Bible goes on to say, this curse ended up affecting an entire nation. I believe these kinds of curses may need to be renounced and broken.

If you are unsure of whether a curse should be broken, I recommend breaking it anyway, so that you know it's broken. It doesn't hurt to break a curse that's already been broken. Here's a sample prayer you can use to free yourself from spoken generational curses:

In the name of Jesus, and by the power of His blood, I now renounce, break and sever all curses that have been handed down to me from my ancestors. In the name of Jesus, I now loose myself and my future generations from any bondages passed down to me from my ancestors!

Again, if a curse landed on you and has been broken, it still doesn't mean you are delivered from the spirits that entered in through that curse. You may still need further deliverance to have the spirits cast out that took advantage of the curses handed to you.

"So God created human beings in his own image. In the image of God, he created them; male and female, he created them."

Genesis 1:27, NLT

The Voice of Condemnation

> *"And I heard a loud voice saying in heaven, now is come salvation, and strength, and the kingdom of our God, and the power of his Christ: for the accuser of our brethren is cast down, which accused them before our God day and night."*
>
> Revelation 12:10, KJV

There is one thing in this world we all have in common, and there is absolutely no escaping the voice of the enemy speaking to our minds and condemning us at every turn.

This is another one of those common tactics of the enemy we see literally in our everyday lives. Let's face it—condemnation is his first name among many.

The accusing spirit is an anti-Christ spirit because it approaches people with no love but with a tone of condemnation. It works through a voice--the voice of condemnation. It constantly tells you how much of a failure you are. It tells you how your heart is not right with God. And it tells you if you don't read your Bible every day, you aren't serious about your relationship with God. That spirit basically convinces you that you're never good enough—period.

Using the exact opposite nature of God, the accuser tears down rather than building up. The accusing spirit uses the letter of the law to lay heavy burdens and crush its victims, just as the Pharisees did. *"For they bind heavy burdens and grievous to be borne, and lay them on men's shoulders; but they themselves will not move them with one of their fingers."* (Matthew 23:4, KJV)

The Apostle Paul said, *"Who also hath made us able ministers of the New Testament; not of the letter, but of the spirit: for the letter killeth, but the spirit giveth life."* (2 Corinthians 3:6, KJV)

The accusing spirit works hand in hand with the family of religious spirits and strongholds, including legalism. Not only to keep people bound but also to keep them going around and around in cycles until they are at times confused about what they believe or perhaps who they are really serving or following.

The accusing spirit manifests in a variety of ways. It can accuse a person directly, it can cause them to accuse others around them, or it can accuse God in a person's mind of not being exactly who He says He is. It can also and often states that God does not care about you — after all, look at your present situation.

Any time the enemy brings up past failures, you see the work of the accusing spirit. This spirit feeds on past mistakes in order to justify how that person is supposedly a failure, even though the Blood of Christ has washed away those failures and cast them into the depths of the sea.

In this way, the accusing spirit is an anti-Christ spirit because it deliberately writes off the work of Christ and the shed blood of Jesus. Its total purpose for doing so is to keep one in shackled cycles and condemnation.

To stay sober-minded and maintain our focus on

God, we must learn how to discern the difference between Condemnations versus Conviction. In other words, who speaks the voice of condemnation? The accusing spirit. Even when the accusing spirit seems to be pointing to the answer, the burden that it lays on the person is overwhelming or irrational.

For example, it may tell a person they must go back to everybody they ever wronged, and apologize. Only then can they be forgiven.

That is not only unbiblical but also stinks of salvation by works. And God's Word tells us if we try to be made right by works, then we have fallen from grace. *"Christ is become of no effect unto you, whosoever of you are justified by the law; ye are fallen from grace."* (Galatians 5:4, KJV)

And getting us to fall from grace (to stop trusting God's mercy and grace for our salvation and justification) is precisely what the accusing spirit wants to do.

As I said earlier, the accusing spirit is a voice. It speaks to us. It may even sound righteous because it speaks of how failures are bad.

While we deem our failures as bad, God looks at them with different eyes. From the Word of God, when we really know and become fully persuaded about what our God has done for us even when we fall, we then understand that what Christ did for us through the shed blood on the Cross at Calvary is the remedy to all of our failures.

What the accusing spirit wants us to do is overlook

or even discredit God's remedy for our failures! Sound like a satanic mission? We have to stand steadfast in the fact that even when our flesh and our hearts may fail, our God is the strength of our heart and our portion forever.

"My flesh and my heart may fail, but God is the strength of my heart and my portion forever." (Psalm 73:26, NIV)

That's right! This spirit has all the makings of being righteous, even a minister of righteousness, but inside is a raving wolf seeking whom he may devour. He's busy carrying out the work of his father, the devil. All of this silliness is designed to keep us running around in cycles of confusion.

> *For such are false apostles, deceitful workers, transforming themselves into the apostles of Christ. And no marvel; for Satan himself is transformed into an angel of light. Therefore it is no great thing if his ministers also be transformed as the ministers of righteousness; whose end shall be according to their works.*
>
> 2 Corinthians 11:13-15, KJV

The whole motivation behind this ugly demon spirit is to discredit the work of Christ in our lives. We failed, Jesus forgave, but this spirit keeps pointing to the mistake as if Christ did nothing to erase it. Isn't that terrible? It is SATANIC!

The fruit of the accusing spirit varies widely. Self-hate almost always involves the accusing spirit. Guilt and fear resulting from that guilt (when you feel ashamed, you'll be afraid like Adam and Eve were when guilt drove them to hide from God). Doubt, unbelief, hate, judgmentalism, critical spirit, resentment towards God, feelings of hopelessness, shame, etc. The fruit list goes on and on--cycles!

What does the accusing spirit want to do? Tear apart your faith and wear you down spiritually. He wants you to walk in guilt, condemnation, and never feel worthy of God's glorious plan for your life. Its goal is to wear you down and make you weak as a child of God, keeping you in a bondage cage of cycles.

The accusing spirit thrives on repeated failures, bondages, or iniquities. Pornography or lust are perfect examples. A person can keep failing but have their heart right before the Lord. They feel terrible every time they fall into that sin.

Paul told us in Romans chapter 7 that he struggled with repeated failures in his life, even as a Spirit-filled believer! A person who doesn't understand their bondage may have no clue that pornography is usually bondage with roots that need to be ministered to and not simply justified or excused.

The accusing spirit, however, is right there to tell them how dirty and sick their mind is. Again, the work of the accusing spirit punishes the individual by keeping them ensnared through the cycle of lower than scum.

The accusing spirit is a finger-pointing spirit, a blaming spirit that specializes in digging up the past and blaming somebody for it. That somebody could be you, others, or God. It works hand-in-hand with a critical spirit or judgmentalism.

Bottom line, the accusing spirit will always point to the problem (even if it's been washed away by the work of Christ), while the Holy Spirit will always point you to the solution. If there is a case of conviction from unrepented sin, then once the person confesses it and receives forgiveness, the guilt should be an issue of the past.

If the person continues to struggle with guilt, then (a) they have not mentally accepted the fact their sin has been washed away, or (b) the accusing spirit is at work. Once a sin is confessed and forgiven, the Holy Spirit stops convicting, but the accusing spirit doesn't stop. It continues to badger the person over their failures.

The accusing spirit also works in conjunction with spirits of guilt, shame, condemnation, hopelessness, etc. How do we combat this deceitful spirit? For one, we need to fill our mind with the voice of God's Word (concerning the forgiveness of sins, God's love and mercy, etc.). We need to learn to recognize the voice of the accusing spirit and cast it down.

> *Casting down imaginations, and every high thing that exalteth itself against the knowledge of God, and bringing into captivity every thought to the obedience of Christ.*
> 2 Corinthians 10:5, KJV

Being that this spirit builds strongholds in our minds, we need to be diligent in renewing our mind with God's Word to undo the damage it does to our thinking patterns.

It's also possible the accusing spirit, along with other related spirits such as religiosity, legalism, shame, etc., needs to be driven out as well. You can tear down strongholds all day long. But if a spirit needs driving out, it will keep working against you to rebuild those strongholds.

Part Two

Been There, Done That

"Trust in the LORD with all your heart and lean not on your own understanding."
Proverbs 3:5, NIV

While I was good at reading this particular scripture reference, I must admit, I wasn't always eager to entrust those things that mattered to me and not lean unto my own direction or understanding of how everything was going to work out for my good.

I intended to ask and rest in Him no matter what. However, at times, it didn't always turn out like it was supposed to. Many times and days, I simply buckled under pressure and fear.

Perhaps you've been told as a Christian that you must learn to "trust in the Lord with all your heart." But this famous passage from Proverbs 3 contains more than just a general statement about living. Instead, you find the steps you need each day to walk with God truly.

Follow these seven daily steps to make sure you're leaning on the Lord.

1. Don't Depend on Yourself

We live in a world where trust must be earned and seems in short supply. But Solomon, the famous king who wrote Proverbs, knew that trust is exactly where we must start.

Most of us have faced disappointments, which taught us we could only depend upon ourselves, or so we thought. But living the life God called us to means unlearning that lesson. Instead, we're meant to rest in God's understanding.

We may know in our minds that He possesses all wisdom. *"Oh, the depth of the riches of the wisdom and knowledge of God! How unsearchable his judgments, and his paths beyond tracing out!"* (Romans 11:33, NIV) But sometimes, trusting Him completely like that can be tough. So, each day, we must consciously lay aside our own plans and expectations—and surrender to His plans.

What if we don't feel like we can trust Him like that? That's where step two comes in.

2. *Cry out to God*

Crying out to God doesn't mean open your mouth and start screaming or emotionally sobbing profusely before the Lord out of a sense of defeat or failure. But instead, it involves acknowledging our dependence upon Him for everything.

Surrendering to God begins with our lips and our thoughts. We need more than a commitment to depend on Him—we need to cry out to Him to show that dependence.

Lord, daily we need you, and without Your presence in our lives, we cannot do anything. Help us to acknowledge You. "In all your ways acknowledge him, and he will make your paths straight." (Proverbs 3:6, NASB)

When we pray, we admit His ways are higher than ours. We show that we're leaving our troubles, burdens and dreams in His capable hands. In fact, the Bible promises that when we reach out to Him in prayer, He hears us. "Evening, morning, and noon, I cry out in distress, and he hears my voice." (Psalm 55:17, NIV) We handed the keys of our lives to Him, and we know He's able to lead us. But for that to work, we have to…

3. Run from Evil

So much in this world can clutter up our relationship with God. John, the writer of the fourth gospel, describes them as the desires of the flesh, the lusts of the eyes, and the pride in our lives (1 John 2:16).

In other words, our blessings can easily become our stumbling blocks or cause us to engage in hidden cycles, unaware we have even entered into them. We think of them as what we deserve or what we need to be happy. Instead, life works best when we remember the true source of our blessings—God—and focus on the things that please Him. *"Do not be wise in your own eyes; fear the LORD and shun evil."* (Proverbs 3:7, NIV)

Sometimes, the only way to live the life God wants happens by separating ourselves from the bad influences or things that keep dragging us down. That works best when we start pursuing something else greater in their place. *"Flee the evil desires of youth, and pursue righteousness, faith, love, and peace, along with those who call on the Lord out of a pure heart."* (2 Timothy 2:22, NIV)

Is fleeing evil easy? Not at all. Fleeing from evil desires or cycles that pull at us means spending a lot of time crying out to God and leaning on Him. But our Creator promises to honor our commitment to Him when we shun evil. *"This will bring health to your body and nourishment to your bones."* (Proverbs 3:8, NIV)

When we pursue Him, we find life—abundant life. Running from evil and pursuing God doesn't come naturally to most of us. Instead, it means we have to make a serious change.

4. Put God First in Your Life

It's easiest to put ourselves first. When something good happens, we want to congratulate ourselves with a reward. When something bad happens, we want to console ourselves or find someone to blame. In other words, we often have a "me-centric" starting place.

And when it comes to money, the struggle is even harder. But Solomon, who had quite a bit of wealth himself, knew his money didn't belong to him.

"Honor the LORD with your wealth, with the firstfruits of all your crops; then your barns will be filled to overflowing, and your vats will brim over with new wine." (Proverbs 3:9-10, NIV)

If we can trust God with the first of our wealth, we're truly showing how much we depend on Him. Handing over the first part of our paycheck takes a tremendous amount of faith after all. But doing so means being God-centric.

To get there, though, make sure you…

5. Check Yourself by God's Word

Let's be honest. We aren't so good at evaluating

ourselves. We will go to great lengths to excuse our behavior, our actions, and our sins. Who needs a defense attorney when we can pretty much find a reason for any bad thing we do? The prophet Jeremiah captures this very well. *"The heart is deceitful above all things and beyond cure. Who can understand it?"* (Jeremiah 17:9, NIV)

If we're ever going to trust truly in God and flee evil, we have to know precisely where we stand. We have to find an objective measure that tells us the truth. And that truth comes from God and His Word.

Of course, that doesn't mean we'll always like what we see or how we see it. *"My son, do not despise the LORD's discipline, and do not resent his rebuke."* (Proverbs 3:11, NIV)

That's right. Sometimes it takes something dreadful happening or seeing ourselves in a bad light before we finally admit we need to change. And the more we're in the Bible, the more likely this is to happen. *"I have hidden your word in my heart that I might not sin against you"* (Psalm 119:11, NIV). When we have Scripture planted firmly in our hearts, God will often use verses to deal with us.

6. *Listen to the Holy Spirit*

When Jesus promised to send the Holy Spirit to the church, He told His disciples this Counselor would be their spiritual compass or GPS.

"But the Counselor, the Holy Spirit, whom the Father will send in my name, will teach you all things and will remind you of everything I have said to you." (John 14:26, CSB)

As we go through our day, this same Holy Spirit

guides us too. That means we don't have to go it alone or hope we're getting it right. No, the Holy Spirit leads us into all truth and protects us.

"Guard the good deposit that was entrusted to you — guard it with the help of the Holy Spirit who lives in us." (2 Timothy 1:14, NIV)

After all, the gift of the Holy Spirit to believers reminds us we can genuinely…

7. Rest in God's Love

When we face a challenging world each day, we sometimes wonder if God even cares. Why do bad things happen? Where is God when I need Him? Solomon reminds us that God never takes a break or leaves us to fend for ourselves. *"Because the LORD disciplines those he loves, as a father the son he delights in."* (Proverbs 3:12, NIV)

Even in the midst of turmoil, God sticks with us and uses those challenges to shape us. When we understand that, our perspective completely flips. No longer do we see our setbacks as failures. We see them as moments when God, as our loving Father, works on us.

And that's precisely why we can trust in the Lord with all our hearts. He cares for us every day. He gives us what we need to thrive. He pours blessing after blessing upon us.

Of course, following each of these daily steps isn't easy. That's why Jesus said we have to deny (or break out of the cycles of life that have been choking the life out of us) and follow Him (Matthew 16:24). Trusting God takes a whole-hearted commitment from dawn until dusk. But we're never alone in it.

Jesus said, *"And surely I am with you always, to the very end of the age."* (Matthew 28:20b, NIV)

Right Back Where I Started

"See, I have set before you today life and good, death and evil, in that I command you today to love the LORD your God, to walk in His ways, and to keep His commandments, His statutes, and His judgments, that you may live and multiply; and the LORD your God will bless you in the land which you go to possess. But if your heart turns away so that you do not hear, and are drawn away, and worship other gods and serve them, I announce to you today that you shall surely perish; you shall not prolong your days in the land which you cross over the Jordan to go in and possess."

Deuteronomy 30:15-18, NKJV

"Behold, I have set before you this day life and good, and death and evil…"(verse 15)

Please pay close attention to the emphasis on the word "today," which appears four times in verses 15-19, giving this text an urgent quality—a feeling of immediacy.[1]

Indeed, "this day" is always the day to decide for the Lord—the day to choose life—the day to begin anew. The person who defers important decisions until tomorrow will be tempted to defer them to other tomorrows—tomorrows that might never come. This road often leads to cycles, especially when we are trying

---

[1] (Donovan, 2009)

to go it on our own.

Moses clearly sets out the possibilities. They can choose life and prosperity, or they can choose death and adversity. There is no middle ground.

Each person faces these choices in ways great or small almost every day. The small decisions are as important as the great ones because those are where the seeds of evil implant. "The Devil does not shock a saint into alertness by suggesting whopping crimes. He starts off with little, almost inoffensive things to which even the heart of a saint would make only mild protests" (Walter Farrell, Companion to the Summa).

Few of us will be tempted to rob a bank at gunpoint, but most of us will be tempted to take advantage of a clerk's error in our favor at the cash register.

Few of us will be tempted to become major players in the sex trade, but most of us will be tempted to look at pornographic movies or to flirt with someone other than our spouse. If we can learn to choose life when faced with those smaller temptations, the larger temptations will never gain a grip on us.

"...in that I command you this day to love Yahweh your God, to walk in his ways, and to keep his commandments and his statutes and his ordinances, that you may live and multiply, and that Yahweh your God may bless you in the land where you go in to possess it..." (verse 16).

A literal translation of the Hebrew begins, "I am commanding you today to love the Lord your God by keeping his ways, his commandments, and his statutes."

This word order is significant because it begins with the commandment to love God. The keeping of God's commandments follows that—subordinate to loving God first.

If these people love the Lord their God, they naturally want to please God. They know pleasing God means keeping his ways and obeying his commandments. Therefore, if they obey the first commandment ("loving Yahweh your God"), that love enables them to obey the rest of the commandments.

Why should the people of Israel love God? They have only to look at their recent history to answer that question. God brought them out of slavery in Egypt and led them for forty years through the wilderness.

During this time, God fed them with bread from heaven (Exodus 16:4). Neither their clothing nor their shoes wore out (29:5). God protected them from their enemies (29:7). God brought them to the edge of the Promised Land and promised they would soon enter it.

How could you fail to love a God like that?

If we carefully review our lives, most of us can find similar reasons to love God. Our lives might not have been easy (the Israelites wilderness years were not easy either), but God sustained us day by day. We also have the assurance of eternal life through Jesus Christ. I personally cannot count high enough to say how many, many times God has kept me and brought my family and me out.

Why should we NOT love God? The most likely reasons are (1) our love for something ungodly blocks our ability to love God or (2) we chose to be bitter rather than thankful.

We all have reasons to be bitter and reasons to be thankful. Choosing thankfulness is akin to choosing life, and choosing bitterness is akin to choosing death.

> *But if your heart turn away, and you will not hear, but shall be drawn away, and worship other gods, and serve them; I denounce to you this day, that you shall surely perish; you shall not prolong your days in the land, where you pass over the Jordan to go in to possess it.*
> (Deuteronomy 30:17-18, WEB)

> *You shall have no other gods before me. You shall not make for yourselves an idol, nor any image of anything that is in the heavens above, or that is in the earth beneath, or that is in the water under the earth: you shall not bow yourself down to them, nor serve them."*
> (Exodus 20:3-5a, WEB)

This priority is not accidental. People who worship God and nothing else will not be tempted to break the other commandments. They will honor God by their daily lives and will treat other people respectfully, knowing other people are also God's children.

In other words, they will obey the five commandments relating to God as well as the other five that relate to their neighbor.

But, as we will see, idol worship will be a constant temptation to the Israelites once they enter the Promised Land. When a drought threatens their crops, they will be tempted to bow their knees to Baal, the Canaanite rain or fertility god. They will see their Canaanite neighbors keeping carved idols in their homes and will be tempted to do the same.

When they are taken into exile in Babylonia, they will be tempted to believe the Babylonian god, Marduk, is more powerful than Yahweh. Idolatry will always be a temptation.

We, too, are constantly tempted by idolatry or what I affectionately call cycles. Not many of us are likely to make a carved idol and bow down before it, but we are tempted to put other things in the Number One place in our hearts.

A Christian leader once summarized those temptations in the acronym SAM, which stands for Sex, Alcohol, and Money. There are many other tempters, of course, but he held up those three Clergy Killers—the three temptations that pose the greatest threat to our ministries.

While the word "then" does not appear in verse 18, there is a clear if/then relationship between verses 17 and 18. IF the Israelites bow down to other gods (v. 17), THEN they will suffer the consequences (v. 18).

"I denounce to you this day that you shall surely perish; you shall not prolong your days in the land, where you pass over the Jordan to go in to possess it" (v. 18).

Moses outlines two consequences of bowing down to other gods. First, they will perish. Second, they will not live long in the Promised Land. Neither consequence was ever fully realized in Old Testament times.

While Israelites were killed by tens of thousands at the hand of Babylonians before the Babylonian Exile, other Israelites were taken into captivity and ultimately allowed to return to rebuild Jerusalem. Yahweh always looked for a remnant to restore Israel rather than electing to demolish the nation.

And while the ten tribes of the north were obliterated, the two southern tribes were allowed to continue. Again, the idea was punishment as a means of restoration rather than obliteration.

Haven't I Been Here Before?

In my humble opinion, nothing can kill or halt a dream faster than frustration and lack of vision, wisdom and understanding of how to proceed from where you currently are.

Frustration means the feeling of being upset or annoyed, especially because of the inability to change or achieve something on your own that you desperately desire or want.

While everyone is familiar with feelings of frustration, whether stemming from your efforts falling short of achieving a set of goals or someone else's efforts failing to meet your expectations or needs, it still doesn't ease the process of waiting. Frustration can be an irritant, a deal breaker for the strongest person on earth. Coping with frustration is all about recognizing the sources that trigger the feeling of weakness or inability to control the situation and using the proper techniques to choose a different emotional response. While so much easier said than done, we still must learn the following.

Learn your triggers.

A trigger is an element in your environment that causes a sudden emotional reaction in you that is disproportionate to the trigger itself. There are some common triggers, but everyone has a different set of circumstances that cause frustrations.

Question—do you get frustrated when you feel forced to wait and do nothing? For example, what is your frustration level in traffic jams or waiting in a checkout line? Do you get frustrated when people do not meet your expectations or disrupt your work? What happens when someone sends you a text or email that throws off your day? Do you get frustrated with difficult problems? For instance, does challenging homework or talking to rude customers tend to provoke an outburst?

If this is the case, you must learn ways and methods to help you avoid your triggers whenever possible. Knowing what tends to touch a nerve enables you to recognize when these feelings are likely to strike and avoid the trigger as often as possible.

Triggers are often automatic reactions designed to keep you in cycles that you are totally unaware of. So, simply knowing your triggers can often help control when one presents itself.

For example, keep your phone on silent when you need to work without disruption. Or get up and take a break from a tough work or school assignment if you can feel it building toward an outbreak of frustration.

If you cannot avoid the trigger, try your best to realize triggers are themselves thought patterns you can choose to allow or not, regardless of how hard it is to change them. Once triggered, take time to think rather than reacting impulsively. Practice stress-management breathing. Relaxed, regulated breathing changes the chemistry of the brain, so the thoughtful neocortex dominates activity, rather than the fight-or-flight amygdala controlling you.

Thus, conscious, focused breathing can help you avoid impulsive action or rash words. Breathe deeply. Before you act out of anger or frustration, pause and a take a deep breath. Count to four slowly as you breathe in, and then count to four again as you breathe out. Repeat until you feel calm.

Manage your expectations of others.

People can be irrational, self-centered, unfair, and inconsistent (cycle-minded). You can always control your reaction but never the other person's behavior—and neither should you try.

Another notable method to avoid the entrapment of being in a cycle is to accept the limitations of others. For instance, say you have a friend who is always late for everything but is otherwise a great friend. Manage your expectation by realizing you simply cannot make your friend show up on time, but you can control what you invite her to attend. If you know punctuality is one of your triggers, then avoid putting her in situations where promptness is an issue.

Cultivate your self-sufficiency. Feeling helpless may be overcome by setting and working on goals in whatever may be significant to you.

Stop allowing yourself to become tangled up with the idea that what matters most to you must be valuable to everyone else around you. It simply is not. Most of the time, it's the polar opposite. This type of cycle only allows you much disappointment in the end.

So, is your frustration due to something you could take on yourself as a short-term goal? For example, if you are frustrated with how your roommate doesn't take out the trash, although previously agreed, maybe you should take it out yourself rather than simmer in hostility. Then ask the other person to do a different chore instead.

Avoid perfectionism in dealing with people. People can be frustrating when they do not act consistently. But that is nothing more than being human — humans are not robots or computers. While disappointing, accepting that the other person is not perfect (and neither are you) is critical in dealing with people. Learning how to cope with any acute instances of frustration is always going to be positive.

Set short-, medium- and long-term goals for education, training, career, and home, and start on the nearest objective for one of your desired goals first. Start or continue on a plan you will follow toward self-actualizing your desires and needs, including such goals as applying for training at a community college and transfer to a 4-year college if that works for your plan.

Be determined to break the cycle of debt by determining to save money to buy a better "cash-car" rather than use your income tax refund to purchase the car of your dreams you can't afford. Then you only joyride in it for two months before the owner repossesses it.

Start a new saving or checking account even if that means saving only $10.00 a month. Something is better than nothing, and you can always increase the savings at any time.

Working on goals for lifestyle-routine can buoy you from a sunken feeling. Even developing new hobbies can help with long-standing frustration.

If you're having trouble allowing yourself to indulge in a hobby rather than work all the time, choose something with a pragmatic side, such as learning how to make bread, soap, clothing, etc. You may find inner, intangible benefits as well as real-world ones in mastering one or more of them.

Gain some perspective. Coping with frustration is about finding hope to overcome hopelessness, inaction and dissatisfaction. To counteract frustration, take action to make some personal advancement. "Action" is literally using the capacity to do something, while helplessness is the feeling you can do nothing to improve your situation. Choose something within your reach at this moment—however necessary it may seem—and do it.

Merely washing your clothes, changing your outfit or cooking dinner may seem trivial in comparison to your problem, but it is something, and because of the way our brains work, each success can bring hope.

Spend time with supportive people. Find friends you can talk to about your frustrations, which will listen and won't judge you. If you do not have close friends you feel comfortable doing this with, find someone who can provide good company during frustrating tasks such as searching for jobs or using dating websites.

Social time is generally beneficial to the regulation

of mood. Even if a problem seems obvious, discussing it may help you discover hidden issues such as low self-esteem or specific anxieties. A supportive mentor or counselor can help you talk through these.

Treat yourself. Frustration can build tension and anxiety, which can have harmful effects on our mood, sleep cycle, and general body chemistry. By improving your self-care—especially care of your body—you can relax and let go of the feelings stirred up by frustration. Merely taking a bath, going for a walk, baking a nice loaf of bread, or reading a book is better than fuming and blowing up on someone. These slow, soothing activities can help change your body chemistry from alarmed and dysregulated to calm and focused.

Exercise to reduce stress. Physical activity can relieve tension and stress caused by frustration, especially if you exercise in the right environment. Walk, jog, or hike outdoors in a natural setting if possible. If you are not used to exercising regularly, take it slow, so you feel refreshed, not exhausted.

This Time has to be Different

"Therefore He says, Awake, O sleeper, and arise from the dead, and Christ shall shine (make day dawn) upon you and give you light."
Ephesians 5:14, AMPC

Have you ever asked God for a "do-over" in your life? A do-over in your thinking, living, giving, lifestyle, relationships, or just a do-over in your understanding? What if I told you that you could have a life-change reboot button built into your lifestyle that can cause massive changes in a positive manner in your life-outlook? Wouldn't it be great to know you had a "reboot" button built-in already available to you and all you had to do was acknowledge its existence?

Well, if you have always wanted a significant change from your old ways of thinking and doing, let me tell you, the wait is over and you can start fresh right where you are. Honestly, no kidding.

Take a look at Ephesians 5:14 (AMPC). *"Therefore He says, Awake, O sleeper, and arise from the dead, and Christ shall shine (make day dawn) upon you and give you light."*

Every one of us could use a fresh renewal in our lives. It not about living a flawless life because that would be impossible to do. However, we can desire a fresh start in Christ Jesus. A new way of living and responding to life's issues, concerns, circumstances and conditions.

Considering a fresh start may be easier for some if we look at it from a different perspective. Maybe it is easier to first talk about spiritual renewal or awakening.

What is a spiritual awakening? For that is what God asked from His people in Isaiah. A spiritual awakening occurs when your eyes are opened through a fresh revelation of the greatness of God (and often after a fresh revelation of your personal state) leading to an inward hunger to seek and follow and experience more of Him.

Spiritual sleep, obviously the opposite, is the process through which the heart grows cold to the things of God. The spiritual senses are dulled, and the person of God and His relevance in your life no longer takes the place it once did.

Now I do not mean a person in such a state necessarily stops 'going to Church' or performing other 'religious' activities. No, no, no. More often than not, those things continue, which shouldn't be a surprise to anyone. For even in the natural, a person can and does sleepwalk and talk! It is quite possible that a person spiritually asleep will carry on with the normal outward routine, although the heart and passion have long gone.

So why does a person spiritually fall asleep or become disinterested in passionately following God? Or find themselves falling back into the same old habits or repeatable cycles in their lifetime?

There are lots of reasons, but one common cause consists of prolonged difficulties, which can lead to bitterness toward God. Over time, the bitterness creates a hardening of your heart by the deceitfulness of sin, as the writer of Hebrews tells us.

"But encourage one another day after day, as long as it is still called "Today," so that none of you will be hardened by the deceitfulness of sin." (Hebrews 3:13, NASB)

Another reason comes out of the slow 'choking' of worldliness as mentioned by Jesus in the parable of the sower.

"And the one on whom seed was sown among the thorns, this is the man who hears the word, and the worry of the world and the deceitfulness of wealth choke the word, and it becomes unfruitful." (Matt 13:22, NASB)

Often, a slow, subtle drawing away leaves us unaware of our true condition. So, we must be careful to be on guard as the Bible tells us. *"So then, let us not sleep as others do, but let us be alert and sober."* (1 Thessalonians 5:6, NASB)

Let's have a look at an example from the gospels and see what Jesus said about 'sleeping' and keeping alert.

> *Then Jesus went with his disciples to a place called Gethsemane, and he said to them, "Sit here while I go over there and pray." He took Peter and the two sons of Zebedee along with him, and he began to be sorrowful and troubled. Then he said to them, "My soul is overwhelmed with sorrow to the point of death. Stay here and keep watch with me."*
> *Going a little farther, he fell with his face to the ground and prayed, "My Father, if it is possible, may this cup be taken from me. Yet not as I will, but as*

you will." Then he returned to his disciples and found them sleeping. "Could you men not keep watch with me for one hour?" he asked Peter. Watch and pray so that you will not fall into temptation. The spirit is willing, but the flesh is weak.

He went away a second time and prayed, "My Father, if it is not possible for this cup to be taken away unless I drink it, may your will be done." When he came back, he again found them sleeping, because their eyes were heavy. So he left them and went away once more and prayed the third time, saying the same thing.

Then he returned to the disciples and said to them, "Are you still sleeping and resting? Look, the hour is near, and the Son of Man is betrayed into the hands of sinners.

Matthew 26:36-45, KJV

The story mentioned above occurred just shortly before Jesus was arrested and later crucified. It happened at a time when Jesus, as He contemplated the cross, was at a point of extreme temptation and testing.

Having taken Peter, James and John into the garden with Him, He asked them to keep watch while He went away and prayed during this difficult time. A simple request, don't you think? Yet what did they do? They fell asleep—and not just once! And if you think that is bad, before you get too full of judgment, I bet you do it as well!

Now, they fell asleep physically, but when Jesus saw them, He knew what they most needed to be wary of was falling asleep ***"spiritually."*** So what did Jesus tell them? I'll put the words in a bold-italics font like little warning signs for you!

"*Watch and pray so that you will not fall into temptation.*"

It is vital we do not miss this point in the gospel. **First, watch.** Keep watch over yourself and your relationship with God.

Keep watch over your heart and the affections that draw it. Keep watch over your doctrine, always remembering swamps and marshes lurk to the left and the right. Watch!

"*Watch your life and doctrine closely. Persevere in them, because if you do, you will save both yourself and your hearers.*" (1 Timothy 4:16, NIV)

Secondly, pray! Pray the Lord will keep you.

Pray that His strength will overcome temptation. Pray you will have eyes to see and that spiritual sleep will not overtake you.

Pray you will not become bitter or hardened by sin. Pray!

"*Devote yourselves to prayer, keeping alert in it with an attitude of thanksgiving.*" (Colossians 4:2, NASB)

"The spirit is willing but the flesh is weak!" These words give the reason for the urgent call to 'watch and pray' above. Why do we have to watch our heart? Because the flesh is weak. Why do we need to pray and bring God into the situation? Because the flesh is weak.

Now, the human spirit is often willing. How many times have you thought you would like to have more or better 'quiet times' with God? And you thought, "I 'will' make it happen."

Did it happen? The spirit is willing, but the flesh is

weak. So watch and pray!

"Look... The hour is near!" In context, Jesus was telling them to be watchful, alert and sober, for the hour He had spoken about, the hour of his death, was at hand.

Now was not a good time to be dozing off. For us, the message concerns not Jesus' death but His return. Keep watch, for that hour is at hand! And, as Jesus warned, spiritual deception runs rampant in the last days. Therefore, don't fall asleep!

> *Be on guard, so that your hearts will not be weighted down with dissipation and drunkenness and the worries of life, and that day will not come on you suddenly like a trap; for it will come upon all those who dwell on the face of all the earth.*
>
> *But keep on the alert at all times, praying that you may have strength to escape all these things that are about to take place, and to stand before the Son of Man.*
>
> Luke 21:34-36, NASB

But what if we won't wake up? In the physical sense, several methods can be employed to wake up someone. You generally start by calling their name. Should they not respond, a light shake is usually effective. However, if that doesn't work, a vigorous shake or a bucket of water should do the trick.

But what about God? How does He 'wake us up' from our spiritual slumber?

Well, He too starts by calling our name. But should no reply be given, God can also move on to the next stage and start a little 'shaking.'

The Bible tells us that eventually, in the last days when the hearts of men are hardened to the thought of God, this shaking shall be on a global scale. It is time for the church to wake up. As we see these things unfold, let us understand the hour in which we live and be found alert. As the scripture says, *"And do this, understanding the present time. The hour has come for you to wake up from your slumber, because our salvation is nearer now than when we first believed. The night is nearly over; the day is almost here. So let us put aside the deeds of darkness and put on the armor of light."* (Romans 13:11-12, NASB)

For this time to become different from all the other times when we declared, "This time has to be different," we must make sure we have truly engaged ourselves. Look at the wording from the Word of God in the book of Isaiah.

> *Awake, awake, O Zion, clothe yourself with strength. Put on your garments of splendor, O Jerusalem, the holy city. The uncircumcised and defiled will not enter you again. Shake off your dust; rise up, sit enthroned, O Jerusalem. Free yourself from the chains on your neck, O captive Daughter of Zion.*
>
> Isaiah 52:1-2, NIV

God is the one who provides His people with strength, but He asks that we put it on. So, how can you put on your garments of splendor? Only by walking in a close relationship with Jesus Christ and by recognizing He is your strength, and He is your beauty.

There is a great need in this age for God's people to be sober and alert. So watch and pray! Realize your weakness and propensity to fall into temptation, for the 'spirit is willing, but the flesh is weak.'

Is there dust you need to shake off? Do you need to awake and rise? If so, tell the Lord about it foremost and believe His promise that He will shine upon you to be what you cannot be in yourself. Let me close this chapter with that thought.

> *For this reason it says, "Awake, sleeper, and arise from the dead, and Christ will shine on you." Therefore, be careful how you walk, not as unwise men but as wise, making the most of your time, because the days are evil. So then, do not be foolish, but understand what the will of the Lord is.*
> Ephesians 5:14-17, NASB

Part Three

Why Does This Keep Happening to Me?

"Do not conform to the pattern of this world, but be transformed by the renewing of your mind. Then you will be able to test and approve what God's will is – his good, pleasing and perfect will."

Romans 12:2, NIV

We're all familiar with the term "reboot" when it comes to computers. Rebooting is a troubleshooting method. When your computer gives you trouble—for example, a program locks up or stops responding—you shut the system down and restart it. Also, a common way to reboot your computer is to press down on the Ctrl+Alt+Del keys simultaneously.

Sometimes an area of your life—or perhaps more than one—has gone completely off track and makes you feel bogged down and like you can't move forward.

If this is the case, instead of making small changes here and there, you may want to wipe the slate clean and restart in that area of your life. Here are some ways in which your life may need a reboot:

• You've been eating unhealthy foods for a few months, so you gained weight and feel sluggish.

• You've been staying late at work for what seems like forever and feel burned out.

• Your schedule is so packed with things you need to get done that you feel nauseous when you look at it.

- Your relationship with your significant other hasn't been going well for a while.

If you feel like you need a fresh start in any area of your life, read on. Below you'll find four ways to reboot your life and get a fresh start.

1. Reboot Your Diet

If you've been eating unhealthy foods for an extended period, you probably need to reboot your diet. You can do this by following a detox plan.

"Detox" is short for detoxification. It consists of a focused, short-term diet that allows your body to eliminate toxins and jump-start a weight loss program or helps you alter eating habits entirely. One of the main goals of a detox diet is to eradicate toxins from your body, which is why it's also called a cleanse.

Wheat—such as pasta and bread—is usually banished during a detox as well as sweeteners, including all refined sugar and high fructose corn syrup. In addition, most detox diets encourage you to eat lots of fruits and vegetables, sometimes as smoothies and shakes. Going on a detox diet can help you reboot your digestive system and set the stage for improving your eating habits and your health.

2. Reboot Your Wardrobe

How many times have you opened your closet and thought the following:

- I have nothing to wear.
- Nothing in here fits.
- Everything in here is stained, wrinkled, or

missing a button.

These statements probably sound familiar to a lot of people, and not just women. If this sounds like you, then you need to reboot your wardrobe.

An excellent strategy for rebooting your wardrobe is to create a challenge for yourself; there's a program called Project 333, Courtney's 33 articles of clothing. In this challenge, people are called upon to wear only 33 articles of clothing for three months. The selection includes clothes, shoes, jewelry and accessories.

Here's how to start this challenge.

- Go through your wardrobe and choose the 33 items you plan to wear for the next three months. Everything you pick has to fit and be in good condition.
- Put everything else in boxes. Seal the boxes with tape and store them out of sight.
- For the next three months, wear only your 33 items.

Following Project 333, the following supposedly takes place.

- Help identify your style — the clothes you love to wear and those that flatter your body type.
- Help identify holes in your current wardrobe.
- Stop impulse buying.
- Motivate you to keep everything in your closet clean and in good shape. (After all, you only have a few things to wear.)

3. Reboot a Room

If you feel like you're going to drown in stuff every

time you enter your house, get a fresh start by rebooting a room. Choose a room in your house in which you spend a lot of time and do the following:

- Take everything out. You want to end up with an empty room, which allows you to see how open and free the space feels.
- Step back and visualize the ideal look of that room.
- Only put back the things you need, love, and use (and which belong in that room).
- Go slowly, starting with the essential items.

Once you see how neat and organized everything looks in your newly rebooted room, and how much space you created, you'll probably be inspired to reboot every room in your house.

4. Reboot on a Retreat

We all need to get away from it all from time to time, especially when we start to experience burn out. Chronic stress can make you feel exhausted—emotionally, mentally, and physically.

Besides, stress can zap your motivation, interfere with your ability to concentrate, and even cause health problems if undealt with long term.

Going on a vacation—or more specifically, a retreat—can help you leave the mayhem of the day-to-day behind so you can reconnect with yourself and what really matters.

A few days at a retreat can help clear your mind and gain a new perspective. Some retreats focus on specific

life areas. For example, you can find retreats for any of the following:
- A fitness retreat.
- A marriage retreat.
- A life-reassessment retreat.
- A career retreat.

In other words, there must be a change of cycle in your life that will bring about a different outcome overall. There is absolutely no way one can continue to do the same old things and end up with different results. (Incidentally, they call that insanity.)

The idea of a cycle is to keep you in the loop and continuously spinning out of ungodly control. All the while, you expect God to make things line up for you when you refuse to listen and obey one thing He said to you through His Word.

A cycle is a vindictive circle going nowhere fast. It is a mindset of the enemy, designed to drive you away from God and give you a delusional belief that somehow, you "got this." In this mindset, you don't need God, believing you can finish everything on your own.

The Devil Made Me Do It

Mr. Flip Wilson was best known for his portrayals of such outrageous, over-the-top characters as the Reverend Leroy of the Church of What's Happening Now and Geraldine, the sassy but proud black woman whose flamboyance, enthusiasm and screeching, high-pitched voice was recognized by millions of Americans.

His trademark quips as Geraldine, "When you're hot, you're hot; when you're not, you're not," "The devil made me do it," and "What you see is what you get," became national catchphrases. They quickly morphed into everyone's vocabulary in the 1970s when Mr. Wilson's variety show became one of America's most-watched programs.

Everywhere you looked, and wherever you went, Flip Wilson was a household character among television. He was well known and much liked by both blacks and whites. When it comes to laughter, who doesn't enjoy a good belly roll?

However, if you think for one nanosecond the enemy isn't shrewd, cold and calculating, you are seriously in denial. He hated us after his fall, since his fate and even more so since your salvation and desire to live a Christian life.

A while back, I read an article titled, "Don't Be Ignorant of Satan's Devices," written by an anonymous contributor. In the article, the writer stated,

Just think in the natural world. When a team is playing

basketball or football, they have a playbook.

This book is to be 100% confidential as far as the other team is concerned. The other team should not know the plans of the opposing team. The plans are supposed to be kept secret so that the team can ultimately DEFEAT the competitor.

The other team is to be IGNORANT of the schemes in the other team's playbook. They can know that the playbook exists because I believe every professional team has a playbook, but it is the job of the coach to make sure that the playbook does not fall into the wrong hands.

The same goes with covert operations in a war. The enemy is not to know what the other country has under its sleeve as far as attacks are concerned.

Well, that's how it goes with Satan, but let's give him more credit than that. His tricks are FAR superior to the schemes and plays of sports teams and armies.

Remember, Satan has been studying human nature since the beginning. I'm talking about the FIRST TWO HUMANS WHO EVER WALKED THE FACE OF THE EARTH were deceived by Satan in his FIRST attempt!

He was good at what he did then, and who are we kidding? Satan can only have gotten better at his schemes with time. Some speculate that we live about 7,000 years after Adam and Eve. Seven millennia and billions of people later gives our enemy a lot of time to practice.[2]

---

[2] (Writeous Rhema, 2014)

After reading this article, I was thankful for one that it was written, and secondly that it was shared with the world at large. We cannot remotely sit back and rest or think we know enough about the Word of God, and we don't have anything to worry about.

The enemy is a lot of things, but "joking around" is not one of the things where he slacks. Saved or not, he never gives up trying to distort the truth of the Word of God or cause us to doubt God in all things.

Lie, lie and lie until we believe the lies of him, and when that is not enough, he tells us God doesn't care about us or our situations. He convinces us God is mean, unforgiving and cannot wait to punish us for even the very basic mistakes. Liar, liar—his pants are on fire!

We cannot be not ignorant of his devices. Unlike the playbooks, which change with every situation, Satan uses the same tactics repeatedly. KNOW the enemy. Learn his ways. You should be able to see him coming from a mile away. And we need to know how God counters any power the enemy possesses. However, God leaves it entirely up to us to spend time in the Word, knowing who He is in our lives.

The older I get in the faith, the more I spot the enemy at far distances. It used to be I couldn't see Satan at work until the damage was already done. But God and the Holy Spirit are making it, so I am PREVENTATIVE against enemy attacks by knowing which situations Satan works best in and by knowing how he operates.

Division

Reading the Bible shows me God loves the number ONE. He likes when we work as one even though we have many "body parts" with many gifts and ministries. Romans 12:4-5 talks of there being ONE body of Christ. Romans 15:6 speaks of Christians glorifying God with ONE mind and ONE mouth. In 1 Corinthians 1:10-13 and 1 Corinthians 3:3, we see how there should be no division, and we should be of ONE and the same baptism, "thing," mind, and judgment.

We move on to 1 Corinthians 10:17, which talks of us being ONE body and ONE bread. Chapter 12 of 1 Corinthians again speaks of ONE body. 2 Corinthians 13:11 mentions us being of ONE mind. Galatians 3:28 says we are ONE, and Ephesians 4:4 again broaches the subjects of ONE faith and ONE baptism.

In Paul's letter to the Philippians, he uses ONE spirit and ONE mind (Philippians 1:27), ONE accord and ONE mind (Philippians 2:2). Colossians 3:15 talks of being of ONE body. And in his letter, Peter makes it clear we are to be of ONE mind. (I Peter 3:8)

God clearly LOVES when we operate as ONE!

All the aforementioned Bible verses prove God wants us thinking and operating as ONE. But for some reason, there are at least 33,000 Christian denominations.

How does ONE spirit, ONE mind, ONE faith, ONE baptism, ONE mouth, ONE accord, and ONE body end up in at LEAST 33,000 denominations? Do you think GOD has anything to do with that high number of division?

Absolutely not. Where division is, you can know Satan is at work. All the talk God gives us of ONE in the New Testaments helps us to know all these divisions are one of Satan's devices.

When unbelievers hear that Christians disagree in at least 33,000 ways with regards to Christian doctrine, worship, theology, soteriology, and methodology, it makes them mock us. They can't figure how we all read the same Bible with the same truths and yet can't agree on the ONE thing God meant in the Bible.

Satan loves using division. I'm sure you've heard "divide and conquer." That's one way in which Satan works. He knows he is POWERLESS against Christ's ONE vast Christian body. But when it comes to many (33,000) smaller bodies, he can work well in that. And he has.

<u>Wrong Agreements</u>

Satan isn't as powerful as we think. He can't do anything to us unless we ALLOW him too. He has to get us to AGREE with him first before he can wreak havoc in our lives. Unfortunately, do we not agree with him every chance he gives us?

He can have an evil spirit whisper in your ear that you're broke. Without even thinking, you'll agree with the evil spirit, reasoning your mind's telling you something true.

And guess what. You won't act on something you don't agree with. For example, I won't murder someone unless I first reach an agreement in my mind that it would be a good idea to do so.

Remember in the wilderness after Jesus had a 40 day fast (Luke 4:3-13)? Satan tried to give Jesus an idea. And if Jesus were like us and agreed with Satan, he would have acted on the temptation. But because Jesus has nothing in common with evil, he, of course, disagreed with Satan.

Jesus was not ignorant of Satan's devices. So what happened? Jesus rejected Satan's suggestions, and the Bible says Satan departed for a SEASON. Imagine that. Imagine a season in which Satan does not try to tempt you to sin.

If you learn his devices well enough, you can possibly be free of Satan for a season. Many of us agree with doctors' adverse reports and decide that because our parents and grandparents had a certain disease, we too must eventually get this or that disease.

We agree with our haters' opinions of us and say we will not succeed in life. We agree with the 50 percent divorce statistic and say it's only a matter of time before our marriages fail. And in many cases, only after we AGREE with the enemy, chaos ensues.

Stop making wrong agreements with Satan. It's one of his devices. Look at what happened when Adam and Eve made a wrong agreement with Satan instead of with God about a particular tree.

WHAT GOD SAID: Genesis 2:17 – But of the tree of the knowledge of good and evil, thou shalt not eat of it: for in the day that thou eatest thereof thou shalt surely die.

WHAT SATAN SAID: Genesis 3:4 – And the serpent said unto the woman, Ye shall **NOT** surely die.

By agreeing with Satan, they believed his lie over God's truth. And that wrong agreement changed their lives and that of their descendants forever.

Offense

The subject of offense is an important topic I believe should be taught often in our churches, meetings, and any meeting of major importance to the body of Christ. I thank God for His revelation on this subject even today.

Offense is one of Satan's most successful devices. Satan can work most effectively in an offended heart. If you are easily offended, I can accurately assume you have much mess going on in your life between you and your family, friends, co-workers, church members, and with your spouse.

I bet Satan used offense to ruin your relationships. Maybe your husband said your chicken needed a little more seasoning. Maybe your co-worker made you look bad in front of a boss by telling her a mistake you made.

Maybe your mother showed favoritism to your brother over you. Maybe your best friend chose someone else as her maid-of-honor. Offenses and cycles go hand and hand. They both revolve around hurt and confusion. And maybe this all happened 20 years ago, and you STILL harbor resentment and bitterness about it.

Satan likes people like you. If you can hold a

grudge, Satan can use you. And he WILL use you. I bet your bottom dollar he IS using you.

Satan always works in an atmosphere of unforgiveness. Yet, forgiveness is what God majors on. He constantly admonishes us to forgive. You know anything God loves, Satan hates.

Forgive quickly and thoroughly, and then watch Satan flee from all of your relationships. He can't work well in a relationship flourishing with forgiveness.

The thing about unforgiveness is you can't pray for someone you hate. You can't love someone you hate. You can't evangelize or preach to someone you hate. So when you are offended by and unforgiving of someone, it's one of the ways Satan prevents God from using you to lead someone to Christ.

If Satan can convince you to live offended, he also convinces you not to minister to someone. And so that enacts part TWO of his device. You may be the ONE person God planned on using to lead this person to Christ. But since you now refuse to speak to the person — and blocked them from your Facebook and Twitter — they may never hear or experience the love of God. You may be the only "Bible this person will ever read."

"Whoever covers an **offense** seeks love, but he who repeats a matter separates close friends." (Proverbs 17:9, ESV)

"Good sense makes one slow to anger, and it is his glory to overlook an **offense**." (Proverbs 19:11, ESV)

Ignorance/Paranoia/Insecurity/Suspicion

I put these four words together because they are related. Surprised? Look closely. All four lack one thing: TRUTH and REALITY. If you are ignorant of something, it means you are unaware of the truth of its existence—unaware it is REAL. To be paranoid means to believe things are real without any basis in reality. Paranoia believes lies are true. Paranoid people, for example, may think the CIA is out to kill them. Or a paranoid person may believe some woman at her job hates her and is trying to get her fired when that is so far from the truth. Suspicion can make you paranoid.

Insecurity comes when someone believes aspects of themselves cause them to be inferior to others or disliked by others. Often, that belief is not true. An insecure person may think she must look bad if she walks in a room, and a group of people starts laughing. Or an insecure girlfriend may think every time her boyfriend's phone rings, it's his ex-girlfriend, and he wants her back. An insecure boyfriend may think that every time his girlfriend doesn't answer the phone, she must be with another man.

Insecurity has to do with imagining lies as being the truth.

Satan can destroy trust in a Christian marriage by convincing one spouse that the other is being unfaithful. He can ruin the trusting relationship between a pastor and his congregation if the pastor believes some of his members are thinking of leaving his church because they dislike his preaching all of a sudden.

Satan can cause trouble between a co-worker and manager over something trivial. For instance, at a meeting, the boss may announce a new policy on absentees a week after you called in sick on Monday and Friday. Immediately you get paranoid, convinced the boss is talking about you. Assumptions come from paranoia, ignorance, and insecurity. Because these assumptions are not based on truth, they can cause a lot of trouble in relationships.

Remember, Satan is the father of all lies. Wherever a lie exists, please know it started with Papa Satan. He knows truth sets free. He knows lies bind and cause grief. So he tells lies. He starts lies. He suggests things that lead to lies. Don't operate off deceit. Operate based on truth.

Keep in mind that truth is not the same as facts. A doctor's fact, based on statistical information, says people with your form of cancer die within six months. But God's truth about that same kind of cancer may declare you can be healed in one day with a full recovery.

So Satan sometimes defeats you with FACTS that are not God's truths. Where lies are being spread, know Satan is at work with a demonic scheme to destroy.

He knows if the truth got out about everything, then he would be powerless. He gets his powers from YOUR belief in HIS lies. When you stop believing his false reality, lies and attempts to make you paranoid and insecure, he loses in his tactic against you in this regard.

"For they being ignorant of God's righteousness, and going about to establish their own righteousness, have not submitted themselves unto the righteousness of God."

(Romans 10:3, KJV)

"*Lest Satan should get an advantage of us: for we are not ignorant of his devices.*" (2 Corinthians 2:11, KJV)

> *And it came to pass as they came, when David was returned from the slaughter of the Philistine, that the women came out of all cities of Israel, singing and dancing, to meet King Saul, with tabrets, with joy, and with instruments of musick.*
>
> *And the women answered one another as they played, and said, Saul hath slain his thousands, and David his ten thousands. And Saul was very wroth, and the saying displeased him; and he said,*
>
> *They have ascribed unto David ten thousands, and to me they have ascribed but thousands: and what can he have more but the kingdom? And Saul eyed David from that day and forward.*
>
> 1 Samuel 18:6-9, KJV

Pride

Last but not least, Satan defeats those who love God by using one of his most effective weapons—PRIDE. He knows this one well because pride caused his downfall. I cannot stress the importance of humility in the life of the believer.

Remember how even the "best" Jews of Jesus' time were defeated and damned. They had too much pride to admit their inefficiencies and weaknesses when it came to pleasing God according to His holy standard. They did not receive Jesus because He required that they humble themselves and admit they were sinners who needed a Savior. Satan can work more easily in a prideful heart than even in an offended heart.

As an example of how Satan works in this way, consider when he convinces you to apply pride to your repentance. You can have committed a sin yet remained too prideful to repent of it.

I personally know of a woman who declares to my face every time she sees me that she loves me as a sister in Christ. This same woman took the time to write an almost three-page text detailing what she deemed facts about me that were derogatory, demeaning, demonic and untrue.

In all likelihood, she will never acknowledge it, never repent, and will pretend she did nothing wrong. Because I recognized it as a lie, entrapment and vicious cycle of evil from the pit of hell, I made up my mind not to become a pawn in the devil's scheme. I chose instead to forgive and release the hurt and rage I felt toward this person.

I acknowledged the fact to God that this text was rude, hurtful and ungodly. I understood it was designed to hurt me and my character with others. However, in the same vein, I choose to believe God's truth over my life and release the rest back to the same pit of hell this incident climbed out of and vowed never to look back.

I didn't bother to confront the lie or the liar. I probably will never have lunch, tea or crumpets with her nor pretend we are bosom buddies in the Lord or otherwise. Instead, I choose to move forward with the plans God alone has for me and hope only the best for her life.

I believed I didn't have to accept and agree with the offense from the devil because I am exactly who and what God designed for my life. Nothing else anyone says or tries to do to or against me will prosper. I choose to live free and unmoved by someone else's opinion.

Pride causes you to deny any wrongdoing, faults, or weaknesses. And when you don't admit to having a problem, you never confess the problem. And you never receive forgiveness for something you can't agree you did.

Satan used pride to keep that individual from receiving God's forgiveness. I don't know if she ever repented of it to God. As of a year later, she never attempted to repent or reconcile with me. In fact, to date, she acts and looks at me as though she never did one thing out of character. In that regard, I know differently. Satan did a work in her life whether she understands it or not. God does not allow for any pride in the lives of Saints.

He wants total humility from us. Humility is not just a cute word to refer to yourself. Having humility means you ask for forgiveness every time you sin. Having humility means you never think you are too holy to make a mistake. And having humility shows me you ALWAYS run to God for much-needed forgiveness. So conversely, to lack humility means you rarely, if ever, ask for forgiveness because you can't agree you make mistakes.

It's so sad to see or read about preachers who are so tough on their congregation be exposed for the wildest sins. I'm talking about being caught having 15-year affairs with a prophetess in the church. I'm talking about molesting five boys in his congregation. I'm talking about pastors who kill their wives, chop them up, and store them in the freezer for years, all so they can have an incestuous relationship with their daughter. I'm talking about embezzling thousands of dollars from members' tithes and offerings. I've heard all these TRUE stories and more. It's crazy how the most prideful, self-righteous people have the most unbelievable secret sins.

That's because pride is one of the best ways to cover sin. If you allow pride in your life, Satan has some BIG, disastrous plans for you and those closely associated with you. Pride destroys. The Bible says that by pride, people bring about their own downfall.

"Not a novice, lest being lifted up with pride he fall into the condemnation of the devil." (1 Timothy 3:6, KJV)

"Pride goeth before destruction, and a haughty spirit before a fall." (Proverbs 16:18, KJV)

"...be clothed with humility: for God resisteth the proud, and giveth grace to the humble." 1 Peter 5:5 KJV)

Distractions

Finally, do you remember the story about the sisters, Mary and Martha? One sister was so busy cleaning and being a good hostess that she missed out on a spiritual blessing from the Messiah.

She even tried to get the Messiah to cause her sister

to miss her blessing. She confused busyness for Jesus as doing the work of the Lord.

Satan can have people so busy singing in a choir, ushering the congregation to their seats, vacuuming after church services, and playing the drums that they forget to minister to others spiritually.

Not to make light of ushers and choir members, but sometimes, God only wants you to "evangelize to your family member." But you're so busy at church the people who are "sick" are not getting a "physician," while the people who are "well" are.

We must be careful of our selfish motives even while "doing the will of the Lord." I believe our God is looking for individuals who volunteer to do His will more so than people who think they already know His will and only want to execute it their way.

If we aren't careful, we can become so busy looking churchy that we have no time to BE the Christian we should be for God. Satan will have you so busy you think you do not have time to do the things God wants you to do.

These church distractions arise from the things we do in church today that have nothing to do with the church we read about in the New Testament. The New Testament church and Jesus were out and about ministering to the hurting and lost. Church today ministers only to those who are saved and inside the church's four walls.

Many church folk would rather hold up a hurtful pro-life sign outside of an abortion clinic than kindly approach the expectant mother, praying for her, asking her why she feels the need to abort, and offering her other options.

Many Christians hold up hateful signs at gay rallies and parades instead of pulling a homosexual to the side, praying for them, and doing spiritual deliverance from the spirit of perversion. Be not ignorant of even this most surprising device.

These are only six of MANY devices Satan uses. I chose these six because they are the ones by which Satan won many battles against me. I thank God for informing me so that I might gain the victory over Satan in my life through Christ Jesus.

I'll Start Tomorrow

"Don't put it off; do it now! Don't rest until you do."
Proverbs 6:4, NLT

This particular scripture is not only accurate, but it is also very open and honest. Why put anything off when you are in a position to take care of it right now? You are able bodied and capable of handling most any situation right now, yet you put it off as though you are 100 percent confident, with expressed assurance, you will see tomorrow. And you decide to take care of it then instead of finishing today.

How many times within the last several years have you said, "I'll do it next year?" I'll take that vacation next year. I'll lose weight next year. I'll get engaged next year. I'll start paying off my credit cards next year. Or, oddly enough, I'll get saved next year.

Sadly, for some, next year was today — perhaps moments later. Without warning, next year for some never comes because their lives ended suddenly. Taken, cut unbearably short because they were too young. We didn't get to say goodbye when death arrived unexpectedly.

That's the thing about cycles. They have a way of giving us false or misleading information about our lives. Cycles lead us to believe we are somehow in control when it is quite the opposite. We are far from controlling our lives.

Humans are notorious for living in a state of denial and content with being in an ill-informed state about reality. I am always amazed at my reaction and the reactions of others when we hear some news for the first time and consider it the absolute truth. We are somehow shocked and bewildered that it has come to this point in our lives all because we put off today for tomorrow. Then here it is—our tomorrow.

To countless people who smoked all of their lives, no matter how many warnings, commercials, family and friends interventions or breakups, nothing quite got their attention until they received that negative report from the doctor. A terminally ill disease, and then, the idea of quitting comes entirely too late.

Perhaps a spouse tried to get the husband or wife's attention, telling them they always felt alone, unhappy, taken for granted, or overlooked at home. They had enough material things in the marriage, but they just wanted you to be home more. Instead of listening, those pleas fell on deaf ears.

He/she didn't intend to have an affair. They weren't looking for someone else to fill the void. They truly loved you and desired you, but you were not physically or emotionally available. Eventually, you were no longer around. Something about being home more next year did you say?

Perhaps you are young and living a carefree life. Sure, you are only in your 20's, 30's, early 40's. You have worked hard all of your life, single, have no real responsibilities, and you're just going to do you. One day you look around, and everyone else is living their best lives while you finally get busy trying to make a life. The problem is you don't know how after all this time.

> *"Vanity of vanities," says the Preacher, "Vanity of vanities, all is vanity."*
> *What profit has a man from all his labor*
> *In which he toils under the sun?*
> *One generation passes away, and another generation comes;*
> *But the earth abides forever.*
> *The sun also rises, and the sun goes down,*
> *And hastens to the place where it arose.*
> *The wind goes toward the south,*
> *And turns around to the north;*
> *The wind whirls about continually,*
> *And comes again on its circuit.*
> *All the rivers run into the sea,*
> *Yet the sea is not full;*
> *To the place from which the rivers come.*
> *There they return again.*
> *All things are full of labor;*
> *Man cannot express it.*
> *The eye is not satisfied with seeing,*
> *Nor the ear filled with hearing.*
> *That which has been is what will be,*
> *That which is done is what will be done,*
> *And there is nothing new under the sun.*
>
> Ecclesiastes 1:2-9, NKJV

How many remember where you were the year

Oprah Winfrey gave away nearly 300 cars to everyone in her show audience? Honestly, who could ever forget that moment in history? On **September 13, 2004**, Oprah gave away new **Pontiac G6** — a midsize car worth $28,500 and produced by General Motors under the Pontiac brand. Introduced in 2004 for the 2005 model year, they intended for it to replace the Grand Am.

Oprah told her producers to fill the crowd with people who "desperately needed" the cars. When she announced the prize by jumping up and down, waving a giant keyring and yelling, "Everybody gets a car! Everybody gets a car!" Mayhem, crying, screaming, delirium, fainting, all broke out around her. One media expert told a reporter, "It was one of the great promotional stunts in the history of television."

I don't know what that moment was like for you, but personally, I was one sitting in front of the television, shouting, "I want one too!"

Even though that moment was exciting and mind-boggling for all of the recipients, moments later, and perhaps unbeknownst to the audience, there would be a literal price those people must pay to receive the prize. They had to pay taxes, and they had to do it immediately or forfeit the car.

Why is it we put everything off until tomorrow? While growing up, when my parents said something needed to be done around the house, the when to get it done was NOW! Don't even think about waiting. One of my dad's favorite clichés was, "Baby girl, weight broke the bridge." Need I say more? If you wanted to live to see another day of your precious life, tomorrow was our today.

Funny how years later as an adult, if I'm not careful, there are some things I really don't care if I ever accomplish—today, tomorrow or ever. Things like my annual checkup, dentist appointments or paying bills. Who's ever in a rush to do any of those "important things?"

When do we start that new exercise program? Tomorrow. When do we start our spring-cleaning? Tomorrow. When do we start working in the garden? Tomorrow?

However, suppose someone came in right now and offered you an all-expense paid vacation home on lakefront property anywhere in the world. Seven days, no strings attached, and they even give you extra to pay the prize taxes. But you have to leave as soon as you received the news. Would you be open to going?

This trip is great. Forget your old clothes at home. You'll get new ones on the trip.—paid in full and yours to keep. But you have to leave in just a few minutes. You might have time to run to the bathroom and grab your purse. Would you still go? I hear resounding, "Yeses!"

Now why do we go on the trip, but put off our needed diet, exercise program, cleaning, etc.? To be honest, one is tough work while the other is exciting. We would be driven and excited to go on the trip. That sounds like fun. Anywhere in the world trip. Hey, let's go. Unfortunately, the trip is fictional, but the work isn't.

In Exodus 8, we see someone who puts something

off until tomorrow that should be taken care of today. His name is Pharaoh. God chose a man named Moses to go before the most powerful ruler of his day and tell him, "God says, 'Let my people go!'"

If you remember, Moses reminded God of his weakness in speaking (as if God forgot). And God told Moses to trust him to do the impossible. Moses just needed to obey.

Well, Moses stood before Pharaoh (who thought of himself as a god) and said, "The one true God says, 'Let my people GO!'" Pharaoh laughed and refused, so God turned the Nile into blood. Then Moses came back for round two of an eventual ten-round KO. We find the rest of the story in Exodus 8:1-13.

God sent a swarm of frogs over all the land. Frogs in the pots, beds, showers, underfoot, everywhere. But everyone else was going nuts. Finally, verse eight tells us Pharaoh had enough, and he called for Moses to call off the hoard.

I love verse nine. Moses essentially asked Pharaoh, "So when do you want these pesky frogs gone? I mean if these critters are bothering you so bad, when do you want them out of here? God can do it now or later."

Do you notice what Pharaoh's answer was in verse 10? Tomorrow! What in the world was he thinking? I don't want frogs in my bed. You think that's your spouse in bed, and all of a sudden 50 frogs are jumping around under your covers! Yikes.

"Pharaoh, when you want these nasty creatures out of your life? Today right?"

"Nah. Tomorrow!"

I don't get it.

Pharaoh somehow became comfortable and learned to relax in the midst of filth. What used to bother him, changed to only a mild hindrance, and eventually, it became everyday life.

But we do the same thing, don't we! We put up with things that used to bother us. To get out of the negative, complacent cycles that keep us in spiritual bondage in our lives, we must start with the things that began it all.

There are at least two specific areas that must be dealt with today. We can no longer put them off until "Tomorrow" when these areas should be taken care of Today.

Sin. When do you want to get rid of the sin in your heart? Pharaoh knew there was a problem in the kingdom. FROGS EVERYWHERE! But somehow, he grew so comfortable with them that he was willing to stay one more day with his old friends.

Have you ever gotten under conviction for your sin, maybe because of a sermon, a song, a Bible reading, etc.? You know you should repent and give up that sin, but you say, "Tomorrow, I'll do something about it."

You know sin can become like a trusty old pet. It's always there when you need a pick me up. It never judges you. Maybe it's an addiction like gambling, smoking, overeating, gossiping, etc. We know it's wrong. We know we need to do something about it, BUT we can start worrying about that "Tomorrow" right?

Secondly, most people think the Christian life is

complete when they love God. Isn't that the great commandment? But Jesus said to love God with everything.

That means the equation is Love God = Hate Sin. You see, you cannot truly love God and love sin. We try to do it all the time, but it doesn't work.

When Jesus was in the garden praying the night he was arrested, he asked if there was any other way for sin to be atoned for that God let it come about. But there was no other way. If you think sin is not that serious, look at the cross of Christ! You cannot love God and love sin. You can hate God and hate sin. But God is calling Christians to be real followers and stop saying tomorrow about their sin.

It's No Big Deal

"Therefore, 'Come out from them and be separate,' says the LORD. 'Touch no unclean thing, and I will receive you.'"
2 Corinthians 6:17, NIV

While I love togetherness as much as the next person, honestly, a time comes when you cannot do, be or go where everyone is going or doing exactly what they do. You may as well go ahead and brace yourself for some severe backlash because it's coming. Nevertheless, you still cannot go.

Now, I didn't say, the Word of God said it, and that makes it God's truth for both you and me. I am in the same boat as you are. I cannot go either, and frankly, now that I have come to the marvelous light as well, I am so thankful I cannot. If you must go, please feel free to go ahead without me. I will be all right.

Seriously, countless children, young adults and even mature adults are afraid to go it alone. They crave the approval, opinions or need to get a second opinion from others before they proceed.

Some remain in bondage their entire life because they are petrified of being, living or walking out their life's purpose in what they consider alone. Even while being miserable, unhappy and unfulfilled, when questioned about getting out, moving on, or changing their mind, they shrug their shoulders and say, "It's no big deal, I'm used to it."

Can I suggest this is a horrible place to be—halted between two opinions and losing terribly at both? You see, 2 Corinthians 6:17 is not a mere suggestion or idea. It is the Word of God for us to "*Come out from them and be separated.*"

Of course, God wants all to repent and be saved. However, we know mankind has free will to make choices for themselves. Therefore, there will be those who choose Christ as their personal Lord and Savior and those who will not.

The invitation to come out from among them means come out from among idolaters and unbelievers—from a frivolous and vicious world. These words, with a slight change, come from Isaiah 3:11. That scripture applied to the Jews in Babylon and contained a solemn call God makes for them to leave the place of their exile—to come out from among the idolaters of that city and return to their rightful land.

Come out from among them. Whatever is proud, arrogant, wicked, and opposed to God and Paul, therefore, applies to the words here. Paul inserts great force to illustrate the duty of Christians in separating themselves from a vain, idolatrous, and wicked world. As Christians, we should not run after and chase such vain things as the world does. Our true heart desires should be after the will and purpose of God and what matters most to Him alone.

While some may find this statement offensive or a bit much, let's look at it this way. God says, "Come out from among them…" Why? Because Jesus Christ came to redeem us from the world. And because our Heavenly Father is HOLY. Are we presenting the image of our Father in heaven (like Jesus Christ was), or are we presenting the image of the world?

"Be ye not unequally yoked together with unbelievers: for what fellowship hath righteousness with unrighteousness? And what communion hath light with darkness? Come out from among THEM." (2 Corinthians 6:14, KJV)

> *Therefore, my beloved, as you have always obeyed, not as in my presence only, but now much more in my absence, work out your own salvation with fear and trembling; for it is God who works in you both to will and to do for His good pleasure.*
>
> *Do all things without complaining and disputing, that you may become blameless and harmless, children of God without fault in the midst of a crooked and perverse generation, among whom you shine as lights in the world.*
>
> Philippians 2:12-15, KJV

Part Four

What's Keeping You From Breaking the Cycle?

hin drance: *A thing that provides resistance, delay, or obstruction to something or someone.*

> *"There is nothing that Satan fears so much as that the people of God shall clear the way by removing every hindrance, so that the Lord can pour out his Spirit upon a languishing church and an impenitent congregation.*
>
> *If Satan had his way, there would never be another awakening, great or small, to the end of time. But we are not ignorant of his devices. It is possible to resist his power.*
>
> *When the way is prepared for the Spirit of God, the blessing will come. Satan can no more hinder a shower of blessing from descending upon God's people than he can close the windows of heaven that rain cannot come upon the earth.*
>
> *Wicked men and devils cannot hinder the work of God, or shut out his presence from the assemblies of his people, if they will, with subdued, contrite hearts, confess and put away their sins, and in faith claim his promises."*
>
> *The Review and Herald, March 22, 1887*

Resistance is the opposite of compliance. Let's face it, no one welcomes resistance into their lives, whether perceived as a good thing or not. Nevertheless, if we don't resist Satan, we succumb to any hindrance he throws at us.

What are those hindrances keeping us bound to cycles? It is impossible to clear them away if we do not know what they are. If we remain unwilling to identify them clearly and truthfully, Satan will work overtime to make sure we don't understand what separates us from God, preventing us from receiving or walking fully in the Holy Spirit.

There is much talk about receiving the latter rain. Crucial to receiving it is first to have unity. But what hinders this?

"For the weapons of our warfare are not carnal, but mighty through God to the pulling down of strong holds; Casting down imaginations, and every high thing that exalteth itself against the knowledge of God, and bringing into captivity every thought to the obedience of Christ." (2 Corinthians 10:4-5, KJV)

The tools for battling hindrances are not worldly weapons. We cannot produce them ourselves, but they are strong in God and able to pull down strongholds.

The strongholds or hindrances that have to be removed are issues with the mind, thoughts, and reasoning, all of which must be brought into captivity to Christ. This is a battle of the mind, not merely having a strong will and includes how we think and what we constantly think about.

The word imagination can also be translated as reasoning or arguments. So the imaginations of verse 5 are arguments or reasoning that exalts themselves against the knowledge of God. To resist them, we bring into captivity every thought to the obedience of Christ.

When Adam and Eve sinned, the robe of light in which God had surrounded them, their robe of righteousness, was lost. They knew they were naked. They had lost the power and presence of God, resulting in a different relationship to God and with each other, and they made fig-leaf garments to cover themselves.

Proverbs 18:10 (NKJV) tells us, *"The name of the Lord is a strong tower; the righteous run to it and are safe."* That was the protection Adam and Eve had in their innocence before they fell. In their nakedness, our first parents experienced a new emotion — fear.

Sin separated them from their protection, so they felt the need to protect themselves and hid from God. In our sinful condition, we invent weapons or fortifications of our own to protect ourselves. Today we call these defense mechanisms.

The definition of a defense mechanism is any of various, usually unconscious mental processes, including denial, projection, rationalization that protect the ego from shame, anxiety, conflict, loss of self-esteem, or other unacceptable feelings or thoughts.

The purpose of these defense mechanisms is to protect ourselves from mainly negative things with which we have to deal as a result of sin. We protect our egos — our pride that lies at the root.

Ellen White puts it this way: we "have many things to learn, and much to unlearn." (*The Signs of the Times*, August 27, 1894.) We usually apply that to doctrinal things, but we have many other things to unlearn, such as the way we think and the way we deal with situations.

Defending ourselves comes naturally, but we have to learn to think and deal with situations the way God would have us deal with them.

It's my personal belief that two specific types of denials make up important words to hindrance—repression and suppression. Repression is an unconscious action, usually caused by a traumatic event the mind puts into the subconscious. We never make a conscious decision to repress something, and sometimes don't realize we did. Suppression, on the other hand, consciously decides to put a situation or event aside.

Sometimes we may procrastinate and think, "I can't deal with this right now. I'll just put it back in the corner of my mind."

That suppression builds up walls. Why? Because the devil plans to build walled fortifications around people's hearts and minds, and he starts very early in life.

If you are young and have God-fearing parents to confide in, you should feel deep gratitude because this world is a dark and wicked place. If you have the light of the knowledge of God, and you understand that God loves you, you are very blessed. Many people in this world do not know that.

Growing up, although I did have that knowledge, I still endured some staggering experiences where I had to deal with things on my own. I had no earthly person in whom to confide for fear of them not understanding or judging my situation.

My foundation of God was where I discovered my safe place. His Presence in my life was my one constant being to whom I could turn. Outwardly, I dealt with things by repression or suppression.

As an adult over the years, I had to pray about many things. An individual cannot deal with something they cannot recall or perhaps deem too harsh or painful for recollection. In dealing with things repressed, Divine help is required, for they live in our subconscious mind.

Proverbs 30:12 deals with the issue of denial, which is basically self-deception. *"There is a generation that is pure in their own eyes, and yet is not washed from their filthiness."* They live in denial, deceived.

Jesus, speaking to the Pharisees, illustrates this deception. *"If ye continue in My word, then are ye My disciples indeed; And ye shall know the truth, and the truth shall make you free. They answered Him, We be Abraham's seed, and were never in bondage to any man: how sayest thou, Ye shall be made free?"* (John 8:31–33, KJV)

Now, this was blatant denial. At the time, the children of Israel were in bondage to the Romans, yet they declared they had "never been in bondage to any man."

Another major hindrance, barrier or cycle is the false payoff one believes they receive as a result of trying to make everything appear okay when clearly it's not. It's called compensation.

Compensation falls under another area of denial. This unbalanced thinking arises when a person focuses on their strengths to compensate for their weaknesses. Within religion, this usually focuses on externals.

Matthew 23:23-24 (KJV) reads, *"Woe unto you, scribes and Pharisees, hypocrites! For ye pay tithe of mint and anise and cummin and have omitted the weightier matters of the law, judgment, mercy, and faith: these ought ye to have done, and not to leave the other undone. Ye blind guides, which strain at a gnat, and swallow a camel."*

Like the Pharisees, we also find it easier to deal with external things, to make sure we dress the right way, say the right thing, and do all the things we are supposed to do. All the while, we exclude addressing weightier matters of the law that deal with the heart.

God gave the Jews laws for healthy living. They were not to eat anything unclean, so they strained water to make sure not even a gnat fell into their containers — dealing with the outward forms. They swallowed a camel — the heart issues. They were self-deceived.

Instruction is given to man how to consider himself: *"For I say, through the grace given unto me, to every man that is among you, not to think of himself more highly than he ought to think; but to think soberly, according as God hath dealt to every man the measure of faith."* (Romans 12:3, KJV)

The next important word we should look at as it relates to hindrances is projection. Projection means to project our character traits, our negative aspects, our feelings, or whatever it may be onto someone else.

Genesis 50:14-15 (KJV) gives some examples of this, speaking about Joseph and his brothers. *"And Joseph returned into Egypt, he, and his brethren, and all that went up with him to bury his father, after he had buried his father. And when Joseph's brethren saw that their father was dead, they said, Joseph will peradventure hate us, and will certainly requite us all the evil which we did unto him."*

Joseph had not given them any indication or any reason to think that way by his actions, but they projected their personal fears onto Joseph.

This reaction is commonplace today. Often a jealous, accusing spouse turns out to be the unfaithful one. As we think, we judge other people. If we are unfaithful in our minds, then it is easy to project that on other people, which is precisely what Joseph's brothers did to him.

Jesus said, *"Why do ye not understand My speech? Even because ye cannot hear My word. Ye are of your father the devil, and the lusts of your father ye will do. He was a murderer from the beginning, and abode not in the truth, because there is no truth in him. When he speaketh a lie, he speaketh of his own: for he is a liar, and the father of it."* (John 8:43-44, KJV)

Jesus knew the thoughts of the Pharisees and their plans — plotting to kill Him. So, convicted, they defended themselves by projecting their evil thoughts back on to Christ. *"Then answered the Jews, and said unto Him, Say we not well that Thou art a Samaritan, and hast a devil?"* (John 8:48, KJV)

Among other things, a hindering spirit can also give birth to what we name rationalization — explaining away or making excuses for sin.

An example of this is recorded in 1 Samuel 15:1-3 (KJV). *"Samuel also said unto Saul, 'The Lord sent me to anoint thee to be king over His people, over Israel: now therefore hearken thou unto the voice of the words of the Lord. Thus saith the Lord of hosts, I remember that which Amalek did to Israel, how he laid wait for him in the way, when he came up from Egypt. Now go and smite Amalek, and utterly destroy all that they have, and spare them not; but slay both man and woman, infant and suckling, ox and sheep, camel and ass.'"*

God told Saul to go and destroy the Amalekites, not only the people but everything, animals included. He was not to spare anything. Saul did not follow the commands of the Lord.

"And the Lord sent thee on a journey, and said, Go and utterly destroy the sinners the Amalekites, and fight against them until they be consumed. Wherefore then didst thou not obey the voice of the Lord, but didst fly upon the spoil, and didst evil in the sight of the Lord?

And Saul said unto Samuel, Yea, I have obeyed the voice of the Lord, and have gone the way which the Lord sent me, and have brought Agag the king of Amalek, and have utterly destroyed the Amalekites.

But the people took of the spoil, sheep and oxen, the chief of the things which should have been utterly destroyed, to sacrifice unto the Lord thy God in Gilgal." (1 Samuel 15:18-21, KJV)

When Saul was found out, he made an excuse, justifying his action.

"Samuel said, Hath the Lord as great delight in burnt offerings and sacrifices, as in obeying the voice of the Lord? Behold, to obey is better than sacrifice, and to hearken than the fat of rams." (1 Samuel 15:22, KJV)

When we are tempted to do something or not to do something wrong, and rationalize in our mind, we parlay with the devil who has a thousand excuses and a thousand reasons he can put into our minds to justify our wrong action.

The Bible says, *"The heart is deceitful above all things, and desperately wicked: who can know it?"* (Jeremiah 17:9, KJV) Our only safety is to stand on the Word of God and not to rationalize wrongdoing.

Traveling with his beautiful wife, Abraham feared Abimelech, the king of Gerar, would kill him to take her for as his own.

In his fear, he rationalized what to do. After all, "she is my sister. She is the daughter of my father, but not the daughter of my mother. And she became my wife." Let's not even discuss the issues with him choosing to marry a half-sister. Still, he found himself in a dilemma.

As we look at Genesis 20:12, we see this story. Abraham lied to protect himself. To do that, he rationalized his actions. In truth, she was his sister, but she was also his wife. He just neglected to mention the part about her being his wife and only divulge that she was his sister.

A half-truth is still a lie.

Displacement is another strong word associated with hindrance. Displacement means to transfer our affections from one thing to another after being hurt. An example of this could happen to a wife who is in an abusive marriage. She takes her affections from her husband, placing them on the children, work, or something else. This method is another way of denying something you don't want to deal with. Putting the issue somewhere else deflects the pain or deflects the responsibility.

Samson reacted with displacement when he returned after being away for a time. His wife's father had given her to Samson's companion.

> *But it came to pass within a while after, in the time of wheat harvest that Samson visited his wife with a kid; and he said, I will go in to my wife into the chamber. But her father would not suffer him to go in. ... And Samson said concerning them, Now shall I be more blameless than the Philistines, though I do them a displeasure.*
> *And Samson went and caught three hundred foxes, and took firebrands, and turned tail to tail, and put a firebrand in the midst between two tails.*
> *And when he had set the brands on fire, he let them go into the standing corn of the Philistines, and burnt up both the shocks, and also the standing corn, with the vineyards and olives.*
>
> Judges 15:1, 3-5, KJV

Samson, in order to deal with pain, took his aggression and focused it on something completely unrelated. The Philistines suffered because of the pain caused by somebody else.

How often do we do the same? We take things out on someone or focus the pain, or whatever, on something else. This reaction could be in either a positive or a negative way, but the result is the same — displacing the emotion.

Another word deeply rooted in hindrances is

sublimation, which involves finding a new outlet to escape from reality, such as a hobby or entertainment.

While hobbies and entertainment aren't bad, obsession with them can be nothing more than a way to escape problems. Today, the devil has made sure we have plenty of ways to divert our minds and attention. Jonah did this when God told him to go to Nineveh.

He did not want to do it, so he went in the other direction. He found an escape from what God wanted him to do. (See Jonah 1:3.)

Looking at a word most people find familiar—fantasy. Fantasy creates a new reality in your mind. When we do not want to deal with the negative things going on, we create a new scenario and live in a fantasy world.

The devil again has many things to help us flesh out fantasy—television, fiction, and all kinds of different things that feed our fantasies. He makes it so easy to live in an altered state of reality in a different world. Fantasy is potent as it engages the use of our imagination.

We should all be familiar with Philippians 4:8 (KJV). *"Finally, brethren, whatsoever things are true, whatsoever things are honest, whatsoever things are just, whatsoever things are pure, whatsoever things are lovely, whatsoever things are of good report; if there be any virtue, and if there be any praise, think on these things."*

The only way we can do that is by fortifying our minds with the truth of God's Word. God gave us the gift of imagination to grasp hold of His Word and to dwell upon those things, meditating on them. But if we are not doing that, we do not have anything upon which to draw.

"It is the special work of Satan in these last days to take possession of the minds of youth, to corrupt the thoughts and inflame the passions; for he knows that by so doing, he can lead to impure actions, and thus all the noble faculties of the mind will become debased, and he can control them to suit his own purposes."[3] (Child Guidance, 440)

"All are free moral agents. And as such, they must bring their thoughts to run in the right channel. ... The first work for those who would reform, is to purify the imagination."[4] (An Appeal to Mothers, 29)

"Our meditations should be such as will elevate the mind."[5] (Christian Temperance and Bible Hygiene, 136)

Blame is 99 percent always somewhere in the picture as it relates to hindrances. Instead of admitting wrong, blame switches our wrong acts to another. This reaction, one of the oldest, began in the Garden of Eden.

"And the Lord God called unto Adam, and said unto him, Where art thou? And he said, I heard Thy voice in the garden, and I was afraid, because I was naked, and I hid myself. And He said, Who told thee that thou wast naked?

Hast thou eaten of the tree, whereof I commanded thee that thou shouldest not eat?" (Genesis 3:9-11, KJV)

They knew they were guilty, and God just asked them a question. He had not accused them of anything, but the man felt the need to defend himself.

---

[3] (White, Child Guidance, 1999)
[4] (White, An Appeal to Mothers, 2012)
[5] (White, Christian Temperance and Bible Hygiene, 2018)

"And the man said, The woman whom thou gavest to be with me, she gave me of the tree, and I did eat." (Genesis 3:12, KJV)

Adam immediately switched blame onto Eve and indirectly, onto God. After all, He made the woman, which Adam readily pointed out. It is so easy to shift the blame and divert it to somebody else, so you don't have to take responsibility for personal actions. Then when the Lord asked the woman what she had done, in self-defense, she laid the blame on the serpent.

With hindrances come advantageous comparisons. Advantageous comparison views our actions against those of others to excuse our wrongs. If we say, "They do it also!" rather than taking responsibility for what we do, we show advantageous comparison.

The apostle Paul knew it is not wise to compare ourselves to any other human. *"For we dare not make ourselves of the number, or compare ourselves with some that commend themselves: but they measuring themselves by themselves, and comparing themselves among themselves, are not wise."* (2 Corinthians 10:12, KJV)

By beholding, we change. Thus, whatever we behold is what we become. If we gaze at somebody else, comparing ourselves to that person to build ourselves up, we are not looking at the positive aspects of their character. And we will be changed into the same thing.

"By beholding Christ, we would be changed into His likeness. But we shall never grow in grace by beholding the faults and mistakes and defects of someone else.

Instead, we will become spiritually dwarfed and

enfeebled. Let us keep looking to Christ, thinking of what He has done for us and of what He has promised to do. Thus, we shall be changed into His likeness. This is true religion."[6] *The Paulson Collection of Ellen G. White Letters*, 318.

Our sinful nature desperately wants to look at others, searching for a way to rid itself of its nagging, guilty heart. The devil encourages many ways to accomplish that as long as we don't go to Christ.

Diffusion of Responsibility, the thought that everybody does it so it must be OK, makes up another hindrance. History has proven over and over that the majority is not always right.

Jesus told a parable about a man who sowed seed in his field. He said, *"Let both [the wheat and the tares] grow together until the harvest: and in the time of harvest, I will say to the reapers, Gather ye together first the tares, and bind them in bundles to burn them: but gather the wheat into My barn."* (Matthew 13:30, KJV)

But notice it is the tares bound in bundles together. The devil is very successful at using that groupthink or group-mentality to bind people together.

We need to make sure we examine ourselves to see if we are using any of these defense mechanisms. As we consider these strongholds, it is easy to see how they create dissension and confusion in the church.

Our weapons against the strongholds are not carnal but spiritual. If we continue to use carnal weapons in the

---

[6] (White, The Paulson and Kress Collection of Ellen G. White Letters, 2014)

church, it only creates dissension. Every obstacle has to be removed. Only when we have unity in the church will the Holy Spirit be poured out.

Finally, a means to ridding ourselves of hindrances is learning how to break down the strongholds in our lives. It is easy to break them.

"Then said Jesus to those Jews which believed on Him, If ye continue in My Word, then are ye My disciples indeed; and ye shall know the truth, and the truth shall make you free." (John 8:31-32, KJV)

It is the truth revealed in God's Word that exposes the obstacles, these strongholds. The truth as it is in Jesus, His grace, and His power that He gives us overcome these things and set us free.

Satan's strongholds are built and guarded in deception. As long as we are deceived, he has us and tries to keep us in that condition. His deceptions are designed to separate and isolate us from our real stronghold, which is Christ. That is why we must study God's Word.

Our primary offensive weapon is the sword of the Spirit, which is the Word of God. It works first through recognizing the obstacles by reading the Word and then claiming God's promises, and finally, applying them by faith to see the strongholds crumble.

"All Scripture is given by inspiration of God, and is profitable for doctrine, for reproof, for correction, for instruction in righteousness: that the man of God may be perfect, thoroughly furnished unto all good works." (2 Timothy 3:16-17, KJV)

God provided abundant means for successful warfare against evil in the world. The Bible is the armory where we may equip for the struggle. Our loins must be girt about with truth. Our breastplate must be righteousness. The shield of faith must be in our hand, the helmet of salvation on our brow; and with the sword of the Spirit, which is the Word of God, we are to cut our way through the obstructions and entanglements of sin."[7] (The Acts of the Apostles, 502)

The first thing needed is to identify the strongholds in ourselves so we can deal with them according to God's Word, His grace and His power. The divine diagnosis to the church of Laodiceans for this condition is found in Revelation 3:15 (KJV). *"I know thy works that thou art neither cold nor hot. I would thou wert cold or hot. So then because thou art lukewarm, and neither cold nor hot, I will spue thee out of My mouth. Because thou sayest, I am rich, and increased with goods, and have need of nothing; and knowest not that thou art wretched, and miserable, and poor, and blind, and naked."*

Here is a church steeped in denial of its condition. God is going to give them a prescription for healing. He says, *"I counsel thee to buy of Me gold tried in the fire, that thou mayest be rich; and white raiment, that thou mayest be clothed, and that the shame of thy nakedness does not appear; and anoint thine eyes with eye-salve, that thou mayest see."* (Rev 3:18, KJV)

The first thing needed is the eye-salve, the anointing to see and understand the heart issues with which we are dealing.

"No man can of himself understand his errors."

---

[7] (White, Acts of the Apostles, 2002)

The heart is deceitful above all things, and desperately wicked; who can know it?' Jeremiah 17:9. In only one way can an accurate knowledge of self be obtained.

"We must behold Christ. Ignorance of Him makes men so uplifted in their righteousness. When we contemplate His purity and excellence, we shall see our weakness, poverty, and defects as they really are.

We shall see ourselves lost and hopeless, clad in garments of self-righteousness, like every other sinner. We shall see if we are ever saved, it will not be through our own goodness, but through God's infinite grace."[8] (*Christ's Object Lessons*, 62)

Jesus said, "Search the scriptures; for in them ye think ye have eternal life: and they are they which testify of Me." John 5:39. As we study God's Word, with the Holy Spirit opening our minds, and we behold Christ in our imagination, we see both others and ourselves in a different light.

Next, we need gold tried in the fire. Faith that works by love is needed to overcome the obstacles. "It is the will of God that each professing Christian shall perfect a character after the divine similitude.

"By studying the character of Christ revealed in the Bible, by practicing His virtues, the believer will be changed into the same likeness of goodness and mercy. Christ's work of self-denial and sacrifice brought into the daily life will develop the faith that works by love and

---

[8] (White, Christ's Object Lessons, 2009)

purifies the soul.

"There are many who wish to evade the cross-bearing part, but the Lord speaks to all when He says, 'If any man will come after Me, let him deny himself, and take up his cross, and follow Me.' Matthew 16:24."[9] (*Counsels to Parents, Teachers, and Students,* 249)

Again, we have to look to Christ, but we also have to take up our cross. As we follow Him and exercise His virtues, we receive and develop faith that works by love and purifies the soul, dealing in a biblical way with issues that arise, rather than facing them according to the flesh.

Then we have to put on the white raiment that the "shame of thy nakedness not appear (Revelation 3:18)." That is the righteousness of Christ, which covers our sins.

Once we break free from protecting ourselves, the Lord does not leave us vulnerable but steps in with His protection. *"The Lord is good, a stronghold in the day of trouble; and He knoweth them that trust in Him."* (Nahum 1:7, KJV)

By faith, we can trust Him through every circumstance. However uncomfortable the situation in which we find ourselves, we can run to Him for shelter. The Lord is our stronghold.

"We need to educate the soul to lay hold and hold fast the rich promises of Christ. The Lord Jesus knows that it is not possible for us to resist the many temptations of Satan, only as we shall have divine power given us

---

[9] (White, Counsels to Parents, Teachers and Students, 1943)

from God. He well knows that in our own human strength we should surely fail.

"Therefore, every provision has been made, that in every emergency and trial we shall flee to the stronghold. … We have the word of promise from lips that will not lie. … We must individually cherish the faith that we receive of Him, the things He hath promised."[10] (Our Father Cares, 99)

We all crave the latter rain, but are we ready to receive it? Is our church ready to receive it? Let us arm ourselves with the spiritual weapons to fight the devil and be ready for Jesus' return. This is my prayer.

---

[10] (White, Our Father Cares, 2013)

Lay Aside Every Excuse

"But they all alike began to make excuses. ***The*** *first said, 'I have just bought a field, and I must go and see it. Please excuse me.' Another said, 'I have just bought five yoke of oxen, and I'm on my way to try them out. Please excuse me.' Still another said, 'I just got married, so I can't come.'"*

Luke 14:18-20 NIV

This line spoken by Dorothy, played by Judy Garland, in the film The Wizard of Oz for me personally is spot on! "While not trying to appear 'picture perfect,' there is no other place that holds my heart hostage like the name of Heaven!"[11]

From as long as I can remember, that name absolutely fascinates me. Even with all of my blessings and trials to this day, I still long for a home in heaven one day.

I could not imagine my life and my soul being any place else. It has all the makings I crave and desire—peace, joy, happiness, healing, deliverance and love. And this list only names part of what we know of Heaven. In spite of possible small glimpses, we cannot comprehend our eternal home.

The mere thought of going to live in Heaven someday makes my spirit in Christ leap for everlasting

---

[11] (Fleming, 1939)

joy. I think one of the many reasons Christians and non-Christians lose hope and sight of the promises God's Word tells us about is because we sometimes lose our focus.

We are all accustomed to promises. We are also accustomed to seeing them made and broken. Anyone who has lived for more than a few years would certainly never lay claim to having kept every promise he or she made.

There are many reasons why this is true. Sometimes we honestly forget what we promised. Sometimes we are negligent, and sometimes it may be due to circumstances beyond our control.

A brokenhearted young lady will often say, "But you promised to marry me."

And the answer comes back, "Yes, but I changed my mind."

People do change their minds, and they do break their promises.

What about the promises of God? How certain are they? The Apostle Paul addressed the church in Rome with these words when writing about the promises of God to Abraham.

"For the promise that he should be heir of the world, was not to Abraham or his seed through the Law, but through the righteousness of faith . . . therefore it is of faith, that it might be by grace; to the end the promise might be sure to all the seed." (Romans 4:13-16, KJV)

God's promise to Abraham was first spelled out in Genesis Chapter 12. It was repeated in Chapter 22. Verse 18 (KJV) reads, *"And in thy seed shall all the nations of the earth be blessed; because thou hast obeyed my voice."*

Now a promise is of no more value than the ability of the one who makes it to carry through on that promise. It also includes a willingness to do so. God did carry through with Abraham. Paul points out in Galatians 3:16 that it was through Christ that God intended to fulfill the promise to Abraham.

Also in Acts 13:32-33 (KJV), the Apostle says, *"And we declare unto you glad tidings how that the promise which was made unto the fathers, God hath fulfilled the same unto us their children, in that he hath raised up Jesus again."*

The contour of Jesus' life, while living on earth, was shaped by his trust in the power of the promises of God. When Jesus said: "I am that bread of life" (John 6:48), "I am the light of the world" (John 8:12), and "I am the resurrection and the life" (John 11:25), He did so fully realizing He had been empowered with this right by the Father who promised to raise Him from the grave. More than 500 brethren at one time bore witness to the fulfillment of this promise according to 1 Corinthians 15:1-6.

What can be said about God's promises to us?

1. He promised to supply every need we have. The Bible says, *"But my God shall supply all your needs according to his riches in glory by Christ Jesus."* That's Philippians 4:19 (KJV). Now notice, God obligated Himself only to the extent of our needs. That includes food, clothing, shelter, companionship, love, and salvation through Jesus Christ. It doesn't include the multiplicity of luxuries we have come to think of as needs.

2. God promised His grace is sufficient for us. (2

Corinthians 12:9) He made provision for our salvation by His grace through faith. Read Ephesians 2:8. It is through obedient faith that we have access to the grace of God, according to Romans 5:2.

    3. God promised His children would not be overtaken with temptation. Instead, He assures us a way of escape will be provided. This promise is recorded in 1 Corinthians 10:13.

    4. Jude wrote, "*Now unto Him that is able to keep you from falling, and to present you faultless before the presence of his glory with exceeding joy.*" (Jude 1:24, KJV). Darius, King of the Medes, said to Daniel, "*Thy God whom thou servest continually, he will deliver thee*" (Daniel 6:16, KJV). He did deliver Daniel from the den of lions.

    5. God promised us victory over death. He first resurrected Jesus by way of assuring our resurrection. Peter said, "*This Jesus hath God raised up, whereof we are all witnesses.*" (Acts 2:32, KJV)

    6. Paul wrote to the Corinthians, "*For I delivered unto you first of all that which I also received, how that Christ died for our sins according to the scriptures, and that he was buried, and that he rose again the third day according to the scriptures.*" (1 Corinthians 15:3-4, KJV). Later on, he added, "*but thanks be to God, which giveth us the victory through our Lord Jesus Christ.*" (1 Corinthians 15:57, KJV)

    7. God promised all things work together for good to those who love and serve Him faithfully (Romans 8:28). It may be difficult for us to see and understand how this is accomplished at times, but God promised it, and He will deliver.

    8. God promised that those who believe in Jesus

and are baptized for the forgiveness of sins will be saved. (Read Mark 16:16 and Acts 2:38.)

9. God promised His people eternal life (John 10:27-28). In closing, let me appeal to you to live so the promises of God will be yours.

The Moment You Realize That God Is Bigger Than Your Mess, Everything Changes For You

"For I know the plans I have for you, declares the LORD, plans to prosper you and not to harm you, to give you a future and a hope. Then you will call upon Me and come and pray to Me, and I will listen to you. You will seek Me and find Me when you search for Me with all your heart."
Jeremiah 29:11-13 BSB

I am sure if I could add up the multiple times I cried out to God to save me, rescue me, keep me, shelter me, hide me, and deliver me, I believe I would run out of worldly numbers within years.

If I could possibly capture all the tears that I shed at just the mentioning of His precious Name in my heart, I would be the owner of countless oceans and rivers.

If I could possibly explain why I love His Name with my mouth, I am sure you would look at me strangely. For all I would be able to say audibly is "JESUS, your Name is everything to me."

Every day of my life, I am learning and growing in His Name. And the more I study His Word for myself, the more I come to understand the Name of Jesus is bigger than my mess. Just the mentioning of His Name trumps any faults and failures I have.

One day, while sitting at my desk and thinking silently over my life, I meditated on the New Year and its fresh beginnings and perhaps all the new things I had to look forward to. I remembered my Bishop's New Year's Eve sermon being "Leave It All Behind."

I thought to myself, "If only it really were that simple. I would gladly do it."

Only God knows and fully understands the true burden one carries and endures, the stress and strain, and the challenges of it all. Then I started to remember this truth. The promises of God often lose their power in our lives because God Himself has become small in our eyes. Don't ask me why this happens. I am sure there are too many reasons to name.

We may be able to recite God's promises by the dozens. But in our hearts, God is no longer the King who conquers armies and cuts a valley in the sea. He is no longer the Shepherd who seeks His sheep and keeps them safe behind His staff.

He is no longer the Lord who walks on waves and calls the dead back from the grave. Slowly, subtly, we have forgotten God's power, God's wisdom, and God's tenderness. Sometimes on the surface, it seems as though God may have forgotten about us, and the wait for His answer seems like forever.

When the promises of God seem powerless to quiet our fears, soothe our grief, lift our worries, or motivate our obedience, we need to do more than hear His promises again. We need to behold the God who gives them and remember God's promises are not buried.

In Isaiah 40, the prophet speaks to a group of broken Israelites. The nation that once shone like the stars in the sky had been blackened by exile. As Israel looked back from Babylon, the promises of God appeared buried. How would God give Israel an everlasting kingdom when they were slaves in a foreign land (2 Samuel 7:13)? How would God make Israel a blessing to the world when a curse had fallen on them (Genesis 12:3)? How would God raise up from Israel a serpent-crushing king when they were under Babylon's heel (Genesis 3:15)?

We can ask similar questions when we remember God's promises from the wreckage of our circumstances. We can look ahead to a life of unwanted singleness and ask, "How can God satisfy me?" We can look back at a devastating failure and ask, "How can God forgive me?" We can look up from the crater of some loss and ask, "How can God comfort me?"

In those moments, we need God to do for us what He did for Israel. We need Him to come alongside us, remind us of His promises, and then say, *"Behold your God."* (Isaiah 40:9, KJV)

Even when we cannot remember all God promised us and our hearts are heavy and our burdens appear to be too much, we must continue to behold our God!

Who is God that He gives promises to us? He is the God of might, who created the world by His word. He is the God of wisdom who makes a way in the wilderness. He is the God of tenderness, who carries His children home. And He is bigger than all of our problems. He is the God of Might.

"Behold, the Lord God comes with might, and his arm rules for him." (Isaiah 40:10, ESV)

The God who speaks His promises to us is the same God who said, "Let there be light," and the darkness fled (Genesis 1:3). When He speaks, stars burn and planets lock into orbit; rivers run and oceans fill earth's floors; valleys sink and mountains race to the sky.

The grass in all the world may wither, and the flower on every hillside fade, but the word of him who made them will stay and stand forever (Isaiah 40:8).

Are your troubles as untamed as the ocean? God holds them in the hollow of His hand (Isaiah 40:12). Are your sorrows as vast as the heavens? God measures them like a carpenter at His workbench (Isaiah 40:12). Are your burdens as heavy as the hills? God picks them up and puts them on His scale (Isaiah 40:12).

Your problems may be massive, but your God is mighty. The sun will fail to shine sooner than His word will fall to the ground—no matter how big our problems.

He is also, the God of Wisdom,

"Who has measured the Spirit of the Lord, or what man shows him his counsel?" (Isaiah 40:13, ESV)

Behold the God of wisdom, who makes a way in the wilderness. The Israelites thought their future as a nation had fallen with Jerusalem's walls, and that not even God could raise them again. "My way is hidden from the Lord," they said. "My right is disregarded by my God" (Isaiah 40:27).

But Israel's exile had not taken God by surprise, nor had it cast them out of His sight. *"Have you not known?"* Isaiah asks. *"Have you not heard? The Lord is the everlasting God...His understanding is unsearchable."* (Isaiah 40:28,

ESV)

When Israel was lost in the wilderness of exile, and saw no way of getting back home, God paved a highway right through the desert (Isaiah 40:3).

No trouble is too tangled for God to untie. No path is too twisted for Him to straighten. No heart is too shattered for Him to gather up and put back together.

Your problems may be bewildering, but your God is wise. He sees you. He knows every detail of your trouble. He knows how to come alongside as you wait for Him, and He makes you rise with wings like eagles (Isaiah 40:31).

He doesn't stop there, but He is also the God of Tenderness. He tends His flock like a shepherd. He gathers the lambs in His arms carries them in His bosom, and gently leads those that are with young. (Isaiah 40:11)

Behold the God of tenderness, who carries His children home.

Before God thunders forth His majesty in Isaiah 40, He speaks to Israel with the gentleness of a mother's hush. *"'Comfort, comfort my people,' says your God."* (Isaiah 40:1, NLT)

God is not eager for His people to be tormented and storm-tossed. He wants us to know Him as the God of all comfort (2 Corinthians 1:3).

If God's might shows us, He is powerful enough to fulfill His promises, and if His wisdom convinces us our circumstances are no exception, then His tenderness assures us He delights to use all His might and wisdom in love for weak people like us.

He is the Shepherd who leaves the ninety-nine to find His lost and wandering one. And when God finds him, He bends down, gathers that one up in his arms, and carries him all the way home (Isaiah 40:11).

Your problems may be agonizing, but your God is tender. Place all your fears and frailty before Him, and ask Him to quiet you with His love.

And finally, we can take comfort in knowing that in Christ Jesus, Every Valley Shall Be Filled. Thank you, Jesus.

Seven hundred years after Isaiah told Israel to behold her God, John the Baptist picked up the prophet's words and preached them in the Judean wilderness:

Every valley shall be filled, and every mountain and hill shall be made low . . . and all flesh shall see the salvation of God. (Luke 3:5–6; Isaiah 40:4–5)

Then God as Jesus stepped aside as a man, walked over those valleys and hills and made his way through that wilderness. He was a man of might, who bound hell's armies and brought heaven's kingdom. He was a man of wisdom, who silenced the scribes and spoke the very words of God. He was a man of tenderness, who healed the sick and heralded God's favor.

And then he lay down beneath the biggest of our problems and allowed them to beat him, bludgeon him, and bury him. But only so he could carry our curse to the grave, sink it deep into the ground, and then rise in the power of an indestructible life.

Every promise from God comes to us now through Jesus Christ (2 Corinthians 1:20), the God with scars on his hands.

Your problems may be big, perhaps even bigger than you know. But your God is bigger, and His promises to you are stronger and surer.

So, look up from your problems. Listen again to God's powerful, wise, and tender voice. And then ask God to help you behold Him.

Part Five

From a Different Angle

"I had fainted, unless I had believed to see the goodness of the LORD in the land of the living."
Psalm 27:13 KJV

I don't know one single person who has not been right there in David's shoes at one time or another. And let me tell you, it's not fun or pretty when you are. It is easy to read the story of David and see how things turned out for him.

But let me ask you a question. Have you ever been in a harrowing situation? You found yourself so worn and torn from it all that you literally felt you might raise your hands at any moment and say, "That's it. I've had enough." Then read on.

Psalm 27:13 records David's response to a time in his life when King Saul sought his life. How do we respond when false witnesses rise against us and threaten to take away our life, livelihood, marriage, careers and ministry in the most barbaric and cruel manner?

In the lives of David and his friends, the king sought to kill David for no reason, and the decision and actions that followed were done most ferociously and painfully—not only in physical terms but even more so emotionally. Remember, at one point, Saul accepted David like a son, inviting him to dine at the king's table—

a great honor in those times. Imagine how much David's heart hurt when Saul then wanted to end his life. It is important to know that sometimes, the people of God are subject to things that may cause them to faint. In the present state of things happening in our world today, we can identify with David's emotions.

Please do not become fooled into thinking that just because you and I are Christians, only marvelous things will happen to us and for us.

Even while being a servant of the Most High God, bad things undoubtedly happen. If for no other reason, we face afflictions growing out of the nature, number, and continuance of the world we live in today.

Hearts often fail, especially when apprehended in sins. Often people cause anger and sore displeasure to others because of their sins and the corruptions of their hearts, thinking no one will ever catch them. Once caught and exposed, the fear of no pardon drives their anguish. Although the Word of God clearly displays that grace abounds for all mankind, sometimes people struggle to receive the true work of grace. Many people question whether grace applies to them.

For those who constantly live in a chaotic, hostile and volatile state of being, it is challenging, to say the least, for them to fathom themselves falling into anything other than dishonor to the name of God because they failed. And then they fear they shall perish eternally because of their deeds.

During times of Satan's temptations, which are sometimes grievous, if Christ did not pray for us, our faith would fail. As Christians, we may feel as though Christ's face is being hidden from us, which we cannot ever bear.

The mere thought of God not hearing or keeping us can cause us to faint in the way of our duty or the course of our daily lives. Without Him, we falter because of the difficulties and discouragements, reproaches and persecutions, which face us in today's world. Sometimes we entertain the thought of fainting. If our expectations and interpretation of thinking our blessings, the fulfilment of promises, and answered prayers had been long deferred, we want to give up because they haven't yet arrived. With David, we have to continue believing in God's nature.

The words, "I had fainted, unless I had believed to see the goodness of the LORD in the land of the living," reflect the providential goodness of the Lord., In supplying the writer with the necessaries of life in delivering him out of the hands of his enemies, we see God's extraordinary goodness, which He laid up in His covenant.

When we serve the Lord, He causes all spiritual blessings in Christ to pass before His people.

In Psalms 27:13, the psalmist believed he should "see" — that is, enjoy all these or whatever was needful for him — all the good things of life and all special favors. These include support under afflictions, views of pardoning grace under a sense of sin, strength against Satan's temptations, and deliverance out of them.

He chose to believe discoveries of the love of God

and the light of His countenance. This belief came after desertions followed by divine refreshments in God's house, from His Word and ordinances, and at last, all the glories of the other world. Faith in these things is the best antidote against fainting when the enemy attacks or tempts us.

Broken Chains & Released Vision

"On the very night when Herod was about to bring him forward, Peter was sleeping between two soldiers, bound with two chains, and guards in front of the door were watching over the prison.
And behold, an angel of the Lord suddenly appeared and a light shone in the cell; and he struck Peter's side and woke him up, saying, "Get up quickly" And his chains fell off his hands."

Acts 12:6-7 NASB

As free children of God by the blood of Jesus dying for us on the Cross at Calvary, we should no longer become comfortable with anything that associates itself with bondage – no chains of any sort.

We must get it in our minds that Christ came to set us free. At least four specific Bible verses prove the same. But first, we must settle the fact that chains are an obvious symbol of imprisonment.

In physical terms, they restrict us, hold us down and back, and signify our captive state. In spiritual terms, they do the same.

While many of us won't experience physical chains, we're by no means immune to the impact of spiritual chains, which harm our spiritual growth. These kinds of shackles are as unmissable and detrimental to our freedom because they affect our behavior, our outlook and our faith.

The Bible features numerous accounts of physical chain breaking, but it is also full of stories about people who had spiritual chains broken by the Lord. These types of chains manifested in various ways — demons, sickness, sin.

But these biblical stories aren't just documented so that we know what Jesus was able to do for people who followed him in the past. They also show us what he can do for us today. Jesus comes to set us free and destroy the chains that bind us.

Modern-day chains we may experience can come in a variety of forms. It might be an addiction, a lazy attitude or a failure to forgive. We can identify such spiritual shackles by assessing whether that thing weakens us, restricts our freedom or prevents us from reaching our potential to become closer to and more like Christ.

If you're aware of chains holding you down, or you think something is shackling you, but you've yet to determine what it is, appeal to Jesus to set you free.

Here are some Bible verses that also enable you to see that regardless of the power any chains have, the Lord's power to break them is far greater.

Mark 5:4-8 (NIV): *For he had often been chained hand and foot, but he tore the chains apart and broke the irons on his feet. No one was strong enough to subdue him. Night and day among the tombs and in the hills, he would cry out and cut himself with stones. When he saw Jesus from a distance, he ran and fell on his knees in front of him.*

He shouted at the top of his voice, "What do you want with me, Jesus, Son of the Most High God? In God's name don't torture me!" For Jesus had said to him, "Come out of this man, you impure spirit!"

Acts 12:6-7 (NIV): *The night before Herod was to bring him to trial, Peter was sleeping between two soldiers, bound with two chains, and sentries stood guard at the entrance. Suddenly, an angel of the Lord appeared and a light shone in the cell. He struck Peter on the side and woke him up. "Quick, get up!" he said, and the chains fell off Peter's wrists.*

Acts 16:25-26 (NIV): *About midnight, Paul and Silas were praying and singing hymns to God, and the other prisoners were listening to them. Suddenly, there was such a violent earthquake that the foundations of the prison were shaken. At once, all the prison doors flew open, and everyone's chains came loose*

Psalm 116:16 (NIV): *Truly, I am your servant, Lord; I serve you just as my mother did; you have freed me from my chains.*

Psalm 107:13-16 (NIV): *Then they cried to the Lord in their trouble, and he saved them from their distress. He brought them out of darkness, the utter darkness, and broke away their chains. Let them give thanks to the Lord for his unfailing love and his wonderful deeds for mankind, for he breaks down gates of bronze and cuts through bars of iron.*

These Chains Must Be Broken by Pastor Joshua Oravbiere

Understanding Spiritual Chains

Many people experience situations in their lives for which they cannot find logical causes. They work hard, but have nothing to show for it. They have it all together, but can't find a marriage partner. Many fail at the verge of success. These are only some examples. What these people may have ignored is the spiritual aspect of the human life. The spiritual governs the physical. When things fall apart in the spirit against an individual, the center cannot hold in the physical for this person. Spiritual chaining is a term used to describe a condition of life struggles that have their root causes in the spirit.

Spiritual chaining and imprisonment may be best understood by studying the physical imprisonment process. Just as physical imprisonment creates physical retardation, spiritual chaining leads to spiritual limitations, which manifest in many physical forms, such as barrenness, stagnation, and backwardness.

Bondage is the primary picture that comes to mind at the mentioning of the word "chain." Bondage has the notion of slavery, imprisonment, subjection, and captivity.

When a person is chained, his movement is significantly impaired. Depending on the nature of the offense, a person under arrest by the authorities goes through a process beginning with chaining and ending with imprisonment or execution if found guilty.

The prison itself, in which he is held, has different levels of restriction and security. A prisoner is assigned a place based on the severity of his offense and how dangerous he is perceived to be. He may be chained within the prison to prevent escape and for the safety of other inmates and prison staff.

This same principle is used by the powers of darkness on their prisoners, whom though may be walking physically, are actually in chains spiritually.

Because they have been spiritually bound, their physical lives are marked with struggles and catastrophes. Their spiritual state is revealed in the struggles of their physical lives such as illnesses, poverty, non-achievement, failures on the verge of success, setbacks, barrenness, and many more life issues as earlier mentioned.

The story of Apostle Peter's physical imprisonment recorded in Acts 12 best illustrates the message of spiritual bondage. This story helps us understand three important aspects of bondage: the road to bondage, the nature of bondage, and the way out of bondage.

The Road to Bondage

Acts 12:3 opens with these words: "And because he (Herod) saw that it (the killing of James) pleased the Jews, he proceeded further to take Peter also, and he put him in prison."

Peter was arrested for the preaching of the gospel. The point here is that Herod advanced a reason or ground to imprison Peter. In other words, without a reason, there would be no prison.

Proverbs 26:2 says that a curse without cause shall not alight. Many people have been held prisoners in spiritual cages for various reasons, whether justified or not.

These can range from jealousy or envy, to outright wrongdoings. In African culture, and some other places, many are victims of household wickedness, having been born in a hostile environment where strife dwells among competing wives and children in polygamous families.

Eating unhealthy food, drugs, sex, laziness, etc., are other open doors. (You will find more examples of open doors in an article called, "We are fighting the invisible war.")

If you feel you are in bondage yet desire freedom, the first area you should look at is the road that led you into the bondage. Unless you address the problem from the root cause, it will be impossible for you to experience complete freedom, no matter how much you pray about it. You must take time to examine your life to find out where you missed the mark. It is easier to get a release where you have done no wrong.

The Nature of Bondage

When they put Peter in prison, they bound him by two chains with two soldiers guarding him on either side. Other guards stood mounted between him and the main gate of the prison.

The main gate itself was an iron gate. He was under surveillance around the clock. Under this circumstance, Peter's condition became hopeless. Hence, he fell asleep instead of praying.

This is exactly what Satan and his agents do to their prisoners. Once they capture their victim, they ensure his imprisonment and chains are so secure he sees no conceivable way of escape.

Chaining inside the prison room speaks of multiple bondages so, should you break free from one, the others might still hold you. The outer gate, made of thick iron, speaks of maximum security – no possible way out.

The soldiers and guards keeping watch are types of monitoring agents and spiritual reporters sent to monitor the prisoner's activities. They have one goal in mind – track and hinder any effort and attempt to get out of the chains.

Have you often wondered why you start a project but never complete it? Why on the verge of success in a business deal, a marriage contract, getting pregnant, obtaining employment, having a green card, writing examination, or some other project you most desire, that you fall backward? Regardless of how many times you tried and the amount of effort you put in, the same result comes out. You did all you could, but the situation remains the same.

At times, you feel relieved, thinking the trouble has ended, only to discover the situation comes back to hit you again. You conclude that you are in a cycle and not able to move forward.

Regardless of your intelligence, academic achievement, and the numerous opportunities that come your way, you still find yourself limited. For instance, you serve under those with fewer qualifications. You fail where others succeed, and people think you are brain-dead. You have lost money and some other forms of investments as a result. This kind of situation can make you lose confidence in yourself so you become hesitant to try again.

Like Peter, you may have fallen asleep. If this describes your condition, there is a good chance you may have been chained and imprisoned spiritually. You'll need to accept the reality of your condition and wake up to fight the battle legally for your liberation.

The Way Out of Bondage:

Job 12:18 tells us "He (God) loses the bond of Kings, and girds their loins with a girdle." The first thing you must realize about deliverance from bondage is that demonic chains can only be broken by God's power.

This is the point of Isaiah's prophesy. "It shall come to pass in that day that his (the enemy's) burden will be taken away from your shoulder, and his yoke from your neck, and the yoke will be destroyed because of the anointing oil" (Isaiah 10:27).

The anointing refers to the presence and power of the Holy Spirit. This point is confirmed in Zechariah 4:6: "Not by might, nor by power, but by My Spirit (Holy Spirit), says the Lord of hosts."

Only the Spirit of God can destroy demonic chains. Your wisdom and might will fail you, and other powers fail you. When the angel of God appeared in Peter's prison, the light of God came down with him into the prison. That light was the Holy Spirit.

The instant the angel got to Peter, he changed the darkness in his prison room to light, broke off the chains that Peter's enemies used to bind him, and removed the yoke off his hands.

Before you begin to break chains, you must first receive Jesus as Lord and personal Savior. As a believer, you can draw God's presence through extended worship. You do so by purposely offering praise to God and hallowing His name, perhaps with singing, verbal declaration of who He is, speaking in tongues, or by any other means, your spirit leads you to use.

The second thing you must know about deliverance is the importance of authoritative declaration. Deliverance can only be obtained by the authoritative declaration of God's Word while the presence of God is on you. Presenting the Word of God is of paramount importance. His Word is the weapon you employ to destroy the lies of Satan. It is the hammer that breaks rocks into pieces. And it is the sword of God that cuts the enemy's chains asunder. God promises to always back up His words if spoken by faith.

When a child of God speaks God's Word authoritatively under the influence of the Holy Spirit, demonic chains surely fall apart. Once you identify any chain in your life, you must authoritatively speak to break it.

So, when the angel appeared and the anointing was present, he spoke to Peter with authority. "Arise quickly!" And the chains fell off his hands. When the angel told Peter to arise, he was in essence addressing the chains holding him to break off at once.

The third thing you will need to know is the importance of following direction given by the Holy Spirit. When the angel commanded Peter to rise up quickly, his obedience led to the chains falling off.

Following that, the angel told Peter to follow him. Peter did not argue. He followed the angel even though he did not understand what was going on at the time. This obedience led to his final escape from the prison.

Though his chains fell off at the beginning of this encounter, Peter still remained in prison. He still needed to overcome the prison guards and the formidable outer gate. To be free from demonic chains you must listen to the voice and follow the direction of the Holy Spirit.

He alone knows how to break the chains and lead you out of demonic imprisonment. He may tell you to fast for a given period, pray in the night, or make a certain declaration. He may remind you of a certain sin in your life Satan stands on and which need to confess and repented from. Or He may show you some demonic objects you might still have in your possession and need to discard.

You may be asked to forgive your offenders, including couples. He may tell you to dip yourself seven times in river Jordan or go and show yourself to the priest to make certain offerings. Whatever instruction He may give, you must follow. Else, there will be no *release from chains and imprisonment.*

The door of freedom is ready to open for you, but you must be willing to follow the leading of the Holy Spirit. God does not offer a one-size-fits-all solution to all circumstances. The specific instructions He gives you may be different from what He gave to another person with a similar problem. So, it is imperative to follow strictly the instructions He gives you personally.[12]

---

[12] (Oravbiere, 2016)

Surrendered Will

The word surrender in some ways means to cease resistance to an enemy or opponent and submit to their authority.

"To surrender in spirituality and religion means a believer completely gives up his own will and subjects his thoughts, ideas, and deeds to the will and teachings of a higher power. This term may also be contrasted with submission. Surrender is willful acceptance and yielding to a dominating force and their will." (Everpedia International, 2019)[13]

About the inspiration for the text of the song "I Surrender All," the musician Judson W. Van DeVenter said, "The word "surrender" as used in the Christian religion has different meanings."

In the NIV Bible, 1 Peter 5:7 says, *"Cast all your anxiety on Him because He cares for you."* According to the Scriptures, then, God wants us to give Him all our concerns, all our worries. The word surrender in this sense is derived from the Greek word "paradidomi," which means yield up, transmit, and entrust.

This word is vital to all Saints of God, and even for non-Christians, to meditate upon because whether we are aware of the present need for God in our lives, we still need Him first and foremost.

---

[13] (Everpedia International, 2019)

To surrender is the acknowledgment of needing something greater than yourself to assist you, lead you, or carry you from where you are to where you want to go.

Surrender is an act of choice but not one to enter into lightly. For instance, the act of surrendering your desired way to live and manage your everyday operation of life should never be given over to someone else to maintain for you.

You should always be active if possible in the day-to-day carrying out of your major and minor decisions. When you surrender your will to someone to handle or maintain for you, in a whole lot of instances, you may have signed up for unwanted trouble on the horizon.

The willingness to surrender means giving someone you know, think you know or thought you knew the power to make whatever changes and decisions they deem necessary. You allow them to play a significant role in your daily living. At the end of the day, you might not have ordinarily agreed with the things they determine best for you.

In his sermon, Bruce Edwards shares at first glance, the word surrender tends to be negative because most of the time, it is usually associated with weakness. The author states that true surrendering requires a great deal of strength. Only when we surrender our lives daily to Jesus do we find life.[14]

"Only those who throw away their lives for my sake and

---

[14] (Edwards, 2019)

for the sake of the Good News will ever know what it means to really live." (Mark 8:35, TLB)

I believe it is safe to say a surrendered life begins with understanding that our lives as we know it can no longer be our will at all. Why?

You can be heading in a direction that seems right, yet be on a path leading to a place you don't want to be. Your motives and heart can be right, but if you're **not** following the will of God for your life, you're not going to experience the fullness God has for you. It is essential to surrender to what God wants you to do and where He wants you to go. Not your will, but God's will!

If I may share a personal testimony of what it means to surrender to God, it would sound something like this.

In the early 1990s, I felt a deep desire to follow hard after God in ways that may seem odd to others or perhaps a little overboard. Not only did I know how to pray, but I understood the power and impact of prayer in my life and to some degree, in the lives of others. I cannot explain it any other way than just to tell you my personal one-on-one experience and exposure of it all.

It didn't matter whether I was asleep or awake. I continuously felt the incredible presence of God over my life as if it merely hoovered. It resulted in countless nights of my pillow being sopping from tears of crying out to God. I begged Him to show me "simply" what He wanted me to do for the Kingdom building, and I would do it.

What I didn't fully understand was "it" wasn't anything "simple" at all. When God spoke to me regarding my request, I heard, "Daughter, you have to be made."

Then, I cried some more because I still didn't understand any different. For years, I was in a state of uncertainty because I did the work of the Kingdom when people kept saying I would never qualify based on their prerequisite and recommendation.

So from this perspective, they readily accepted the gift but could often care less about the giver who often labored when others did not want to accept the challenge nor showed any interest in getting the work done.

Over the years of serving, I was overlooked, talked about, laughed at, said I couldn't do it because I was a woman, that I needed validation and approval from others. But God!

Many days, I felt like enough was enough, and I wanted to quit. When I thought it was over in terms of ministry being the place I was headed, I moved toward contentment with the basics of keeping a low profile.

The more I tried to stay away from reaching out to God for more and being content over where I was, the more the presence of God charged after me.

Finally, I simply prayed, "God, please take away my longing and desire for more of You and allow me to be "normal" where I am. I no longer want the desire to minister to Your people or teach Your Word with such a drive and hunger." Because of the coldness from people, the hurtful words they said behind my back, or the pastors who didn't think I belonged or was qualified to do so, I almost gave up.

It was only then that I heard, "Daughter, you have to be made."

What? Wasn't I already saved, I thought?

"Yes, but you have to be made in order to carry out the work that I have prepared for you."

As I continue to grow in Christ, I am learning what those words meant. I needed to have a surrendered life before Him. Fully persuaded. Fully committed, unregrettably yielded unto Him and not held captive by humanity.

Finally, I surrendered and said yes to His will for my life.

Over the next few years, as I shared what I believed God called me to do, I received mixed responses. Not everyone was excited or understood why or what I was about to do. For some, that meant some of the dynamics of my life as they knew me were changing for my good but not readily understood or acceptable for them.

I remember, on one occasion, I was working and had a wonderful job with great benefits when someone gave me a prophetic word that I would be moved from that job and given a heart after ministry.

I thought, "No, this cannot be true. No way. This cannot be God's will for my life."

But no matter how much I fought, it turns out the prophetic word was exactly the direction in which God was taking me. With no apparent means of income, at the end of the two weeks' notice, I trusted God and launched out into the deep.

While nothing made sense in the natural, it came

down to making a choice—not my will, but His will be done. It meant surrendering.

You may ask, "What kind of sense did this make?"

Great question. None in the natural. However, I learned a long time ago, God never makes sense, but He alone makes wisdom!

Jesus is our Supreme Example of Surrendering to the will of God. The night before his crucifixion, Jesus surrendered himself to God's plan. He prayed, *"Father, everything is possible for you. Please take this cup of suffering away from me. Yet I want your will, not mine."* (Mark 14:36, NLT)

Jesus surrendered himself to God's will.

Surrender seldom comes easy. Jesus agonized over God's plan so much that he sweated drops of blood. He did not want to go through the rejection and pain He was about to endure. However, Jesus ended His prayer with, "… not as I will, but as You will."

Surrendering brings life and blessings to others. Refusing to surrender leads us astray and away from God's perfect will and plan. When we surrender, it not only brings victory into our life, but it also has a significant impact on the kingdom of God. Jesus' obedience and surrender brought salvation to you, me and all the world.

My decision to surrender to the will of God wasn't easy. It required hard work and faith. However, it brought great satisfaction and victory for our family and allowed us to be part of things we never imagined – helping build the kingdom of God. All the glory goes to

Him. Surrender is only accomplished by His grace and the Holy Spirit.

Never forget that our surrendering is a choice we have to make. You may be in a situation of weighing God's will for your life. You know in your heart what to do, but your mind and others' words keep fighting you.

Choose to surrender to God. NOT YOUR WILL, BUT HIS WILL BE DONE! When you surrender your will to God's, not only do you find life, but others will be blessed because of your surrender and obedience to God.

Keep in mind, surrender is not a one-time experience. Every day we must choose to surrender to His will for our life on some level. What happens when you do?

1) You grow closer to Him. Psalm 73:28 (KJV) – *"But it is good for me to draw near to God; I have put my trust in the Lord God, that I may declare all Your works."*

2) You hear His voice more clearly. John 10:3-4 (NASB) – *"To him the doorkeeper opens, and the sheep hear his voice; and he calls his own sheep by name and leads them out. And when he brings out his own sheep, he goes before them, and the sheep follow him, for they know his voice."*

3) His Spirit leads you. Romans 8:14 (BLB) – *"For as many as are led by the Spirit of God, these are Sons of God."*

4) You walk in His authority over evil. Luke 10:17 – 19 (NKJV) – *"Then the seventy returned with joy, saying, 'Lord, even the demons are subject to us in Your name.' And He said to them, 'I saw Satan fall like lightning from heaven. Behold, I give you the authority to trample on serpents and scorpions, and over all the power of the enemy, and nothing shall by any means hurt you.'"*

5) He enlarges your vision. Ephesians 3:14-19 (NKJV) – *"For this reason I bow my knees to the Father of our Lord Jesus Christ, from whom the whole family in heaven and earth is named, that He would grant you, according to the riches of His glory, to be strengthened with might through His Spirit in the inner man. That Christ may dwell in your hearts through faith; that you, being rooted and grounded in love, may be able to comprehend with all the saints what is the width and length and depth and height – to know the love of Christ which passes knowledge; that you may be filled with all the fullness of God."*

Choose to surrender your will and find life!

Gracious Grace

*"The definition of grace is **God's unmerited, undeserved, and unearned favor, and our faith in it gives us access to it.** When we truly believe in our hearts that God wants this kind of grace-based prosperity for us, it will eventually come to pass."*

~Creflo Dollar[15]

Depending on who you listen to, grace can be described in multiple ways. Grace, which comes from the Greek New Testament word *charis*, generally means God's unmerited favor. **It is kindness from God we don't deserve.**

There is nothing we have done, nor can ever do, to earn this favor. It is a gift from God. While I don't know how you feel about this, I learned how to be grateful and not ask too many questions.

I am learning so many incredible things about the gracious hand of God through personal life experiences. Some are too amazing to put into words, but I will try my best to elaborate on a few.

This particular passage of scripture ministered to me when I was at my lowest. To this day, I will never forget its presence in my life. We indeed serve an Awesome, Compassionate and Loving God.

---

[15] (Dollar, 2016)

Nehemiah Inspects the Walls

Then I said to them, "You see the trouble we are in. Jerusalem lies in ruins, and its gates have been burned down. Come, let us rebuild the wall of Jerusalem, so that we will no longer be a disgrace." I also told them about the gracious hand of my God upon me, and what the king had said to me. "Let us start rebuilding," they replied, and they set their hands to this good work. When Sanballat the Horonite, Tobiah the Ammonite official, and Geshem the Arab heard about this, they mocked us and ridiculed us, saying, "What is this you are doing? Are you rebelling against the king?"

Nehemiah 2:17-19, BSB

Gracious people are kind, and their behavior characterized by tact. Graciousness may be superficial, but sometimes what we see on the surface is good enough.

A gracious person is a graceful person, someone who at least attempts not to hurt others' feelings with clumsy words or thoughtless deeds. To live in grace aims to walk lightly and leave the world blessed by your presence.

Our God is Gracious. To be gracious implies favor, showing kindnesses to an inferior, and compassion. In the Old Testament of the Bible, this adjective applies to God, indicative of His favor and mercy, His long-suffering and general inclination of favor and kindness.

*The prophet Isaiah wrote, "**Yet the Lord longs to be gracious to you; therefore he will rise up to show you compassion.**" (Isaiah 30:18a NIV)*

God is gracious because He is love. True to His character, God loves even if we don't return that love. He gives us good things because of His goodness. He extends favor, mercy, and kindness on whomever He pleases because it's who He is.

God is gracious because He is our Creator. Even when we don't acknowledge Him or worship Him, He still endows us with good things because He wants to. God created humanity as good, and He won't turn His back on His creation.

"Grace is another attribute that is part of the manifold of God's love. By this we mean that God deals with his people not on the basis of their merit or worthiness, what they deserve, but simply according to their need; in other words, he deals with them on the basis of his goodness and generosity." [16]

You may ask, "How is God gracious?"

Think of a parent. A father and mother give good things to their children because they want to nurture them, never considering worthiness. They provide shelter, food, and clothing because they know these things are necessary for the well-being of the children. They also give gifts out of love with no reason or strings attached.

---

[16] (Erickson, 2013)

God does the same thing. He provided everything for humanity, so we grow and prosper. Yet, He goes beyond subsistence. He personalizes every gift. He does this even though we don't recognize or deserve it.

Ephesians 1:7-8 (NIV) shows God's grace. *"In him we have redemption through his blood, the forgiveness of sins, in accordance with the riches of God's grace that he lavished on us with all wisdom and understanding."*

Through the sacrifice of His Son, Jesus, on the cross, we received His grace.

When is God gracious? Perhaps a better question is, "When is God not gracious?" God is gracious all the time, even when we are disobedient to Him. It is His character to be gracious, and He "*does not change like the shifting shadows*" (James 1:17, NIV). He extends His mercy to us until the final moment of our lives. He wants none to perish because He created us to live in eternity with Him.

By God's grace alone, we can have eternal life. God had so much compassion on humanity that He sent His only Son to die for the disobedience of all mankind. God is gracious in our times of need, sending provision for us.

> *"For it is by grace you have been saved, through faith – and this is not from yourselves, it is the gift of God – not by works, so that no one can boast. For we are God's handiwork, created in Christ Jesus to do good works, which God prepared in advance for us to do"*
>
> (Ephesians 2:8-10, NIV)

> *"Therefore, since we have been justified through faith,*

we have peace with God through our Lord Jesus Christ, through whom we have gained access by faith into this grace in which we now stand. And we boast in the hope of the glory of God."

(Romans 5:1-2, NIV)

We extend God's grace to those in need by extending our hands on His behalf. We help our brothers and sisters in this world to find peace, comfort, and strength in times when desperation threatens to overwhelm them. God desires us to have this response to each other.

As we seek God for who He is, we gain understanding and wisdom. He then begins to mold us into a likeness of His son, Jesus. Our character changes, and we become more willing to show God's grace and kindness to the world.

Conclusion – The Leading of the Good Shepherd

"He makes me lie down in green pastures, he leads me beside quiet waters"
                                                     Psalm 23:2, NIV

We understand the role of Shepherd can apply in several different ways, such as the following.

A. A pastor is a shepherd to the church.

B. An elder or deacon is a shepherd within the body.

C. A husband is a shepherd to his wife.

D. Parents are shepherds to their children.

E. A teacher is a shepherd to his students.

F. An employer is a shepherd to his employees.

G. An older child is a shepherd to his younger brothers and sisters.

H. Anyone who leads someone in any way is a shepherd, responsible for the care of another.

But make no mistake, there is only One Good Shepherd, and His Name is Jesus.

Likewise, we should understand the LORD (Yahweh) is the good shepherd David speaks of in the Psalm. We should also understand that Jesus declares he is the good shepherd, thus making him God.

"I am the good shepherd: the good shepherd giveth his life for the sheep." (John 10:11, KJV) However, let us not

overlook the truth of a good shepherd as we reflect on the characteristics of The Good Shepherd and how He cares for us in that role.

What are the responsibilities of the good shepherd? First and most important, He should know His sheep. "*I am the good shepherd, and know my sheep, and am known of mine.*" (John 10:14, KJV) Note the word "know" is the same word used of the intimate knowing of man and wife.

Not only should the good shepherd know his sheep but it is vital that He knows them intimately, He knows them by name. "*To him the porter openeth; and the sheep hear his voice: and he calleth his own sheep by name, and leadeth them out.*" (John 10:3, KJV) And because of this, He provides a deep sense of belonging.

Because He is recognized as the Good Shepherd, according to Psalm 23:1, they shall not want for NO thing. "I shall not want." Additionally, the shepherd has to have keen eyesight and insight of his sheep. Therefore, the shepherd should see that the needs of the sheep are met.

How does He manage that need? He **feeds** the sheep. "*So when they had dined, Jesus saith to Simon Peter, Simon, son of Jonas, lovest thou me more than these? He saith unto him, Yea, Lord; thou knowest that I love thee. He saith unto him, Feed my lambs. He saith to him again the second time, Simon, son of Jonas, lovest thou me? He saith unto him, Yea, Lord; thou knowest that I love thee. He saith unto him, Feed my sheep. He saith unto him the third time, Simon, son of Jonas, lovest thou me? Peter was grieved because he said unto him the third time, Lovest thou me? And he said unto* *him, Lord, thou knowest all things; thou knowest that I love thee. Jesus saith unto him, Feed my sheep."* (John 21:15-17, KJV)

Jesus asked, "Do you **love me** more than these? (The Greek word for love, (agape) means a self-giving type of love. But that wasn't the word Peter used.)

Peter responded, "I **have affection** for you like a brother." (He used the Greek word "phileo," meaning to have affection for a brother.)

Jesus said, "Feed my lambs."

Jesus asked a second time, "Do you **love** me?"

Peter again responded, "Yes, Lord, you know I **have affection** for you as a brother."

Jesus said, "Shepherd (or tend to) my sheep."

Jesus asked the third time, "Do you **have affection** for me as a brother?" (Note, Jesus changed his wording to meet Peter where he lived in the moment.)

This time Peter responded, "You know that I **have affection** for you."

Jesus said, "Feed my sheep."

As a good shepherd, the question arises. How much affection is shown toward the sheep you care for? Do you love your sheep enough to feed the young lambs using a bottle, tend to the needs of the sheep, and feed the older sheep as well?

Jesus' replies through Psalm 23: 2 (KJV),*"He maketh me to lie down in green pastures."* Green pastures pictures a place of tranquility and a soft bed of grass. Green pastures are a place of rest. The shepherd should not be a slave driver, but one who provides rest for his sheep.

We should not treat our sheep as dogs, telling them they must fetch this, that or the other for us all the time.

Psalm 23:2 (KJV) *"He leadeth me beside the still waters."* The shepherd is to lead his sheep, not drive them. *"My sheep hear my voice, and I know them, and they follow me"* (John 10:27, KJV). The sheep should be able to trust the voice of the shepherd and be willing to follow him.

"The elders which are among you I exhort, who am also an elder, and a witness of the sufferings of Christ, and also a partaker of the glory that shall be revealed:

Feed the flock of God, which is among you, taking the oversight thereof, not by constraint, but willingly; not for filthy lucre, but of a ready mind; Neither as being lords over God's heritage, but being ensamples to the flock. And when the chief Shepherd shall appear, ye shall receive a crown of glory that fadeth not away." (I Peter 5:1-4, KJV)

A. Again the shepherd is to care for the sheep (not just feed them).

B. God has given you that role and position of a shepherd.

C. We should not do it out of compulsion, but voluntarily.

D. We should not do it for money, but willingly.

E. We should not be lords over the sheep but lead by being examples to the flock.

If we are willing to do these things, we can expect to receive the crown of glory.

Whereby the good shepherd leads his sheep by still water where there is no fear of drowning because the shepherd promises to restore our souls—a promise that ensures our soul (which is the mind, will and emotions) is whole because he affirms the sheep rather than bring criticism.

He encourages the sheep rather than discouraging them. He instructs rather than condemns them. He speaks blessings over them rather than cursing them. He protects them rather than feeding them to the wolves. He gathers them together with the flock rather than scattering them in the wilderness. Shepherds are to bring healing.

Also, our good Shepherd is one who goes looking for the lost sheep.

> *And he spake this parable unto them, saying, What man of you, having an hundred sheep, if he lose one of them, doth not leave the ninety and nine in the wilderness, and go after that which is lost, until he find it?*
> *And when he hath found it, he layeth it on his shoulders, rejoicing. And when he cometh home, he calleth together his friends and neighbours, saying unto them, Rejoice with me; for I have found my sheep which was lost. I say unto you, that likewise joy shall be in heaven over one sinner that repenteth, more than over ninety and nine just persons, which need no repentance.*
>
> Luke 15:3-7, KJV

The shepherd leaves the flock to go after the one that is lost, searching until he finds it. He brings it back upon his shoulders, rejoicing. He carries it, so the wayward sheep becomes dependent on the shepherd and the flock. He celebrates that he found it.

He lovingly disciplines the sheep. "*He that spareth his rod hateth his son: but he that loveth him chasteneth him betimes.*" (Proverbs 13:24, KJV)

The shepherd should also realize <u>his reputation</u> is at stake. Therefore in Psalm 23:4 (KJV), the writer states, "*Yea, though I walk through the valley of the shadow of death, I will fear no evil: for thou art with me; thy rod and thy staff they comfort me.*"

The shepherd provides security for the sheep delivering freedom from fear for the sheep. The good shepherd must be willing to give his life for the flock.

"*I am the good shepherd: the good shepherd giveth his life for the sheep.*" (John 10:11, KJV)

The shepherd should be willing to stay with his sheep instead of running away in fear, leaving them to the wolf.

"*But he that is an hireling, and not the shepherd, whose own the sheep are not, seeth the wolf coming, and leaveth the sheep, and fleeth: and the wolf catcheth them, and scattereth the sheep. The hireling fleeth, because he is an hireling, and careth not for the sheep.*" (John 10:12-13, KJV)

The rod represents the authority of the shepherd. A rod during Old Testament times was a club the shepherd used to protect his sheep. The staff was a long stick with a hook on the end, used as an aid to pull the sheep out of the pit if it fell into one. He carried them because a shepherd must be willing to fight for his sheep.

> *And David said to Saul, "Let no man's heart fail because of him; thy servant will go and fight with this Philistine."*
> *And Saul said to David, "Thou art not able to go against this Philistine to fight with him: for thou art but a youth, and he a man of war from his youth."*
> *And David said unto Saul, "Thy servant kept his father's sheep, and there came a lion, and a bear, and took a lamb out of the flock: And I went out after him, and smote him, and delivered it out of his mouth: and when he arose against me, I caught him by his beard, and smote him, and slew him.*
> *Thy servant slew both the lion and the bear: and this uncircumcised Philistine shall be as one of them, seeing he hath defied the armies of the living God."*
>
> I Samuel 17:32-36, KJV

His first concern was for the sheep. "*Thou preparest a table before me in the presence of mine enemies.*" The shepherd must prepare the food for the sheep. The shepherd must prepare the field. He must remove the stones and thorn bushes. He may also need to cultivate and irrigate the field and build a hedge around it.

He must spend time in the Word. If a shepherd does not study the Word, he has nothing to share with his sheep. If the shepherd properly feeds the sheep, they will grow **strong** and **healthy** and then **multiply**.

"*Study to shew thyself approved unto God, a workman that needeth not to be ashamed, rightly dividing the word of truth.*" (2 Timothy 2:15, KJV)

"*Thou anointest my head with oil.*" The anointing is to

bring a sense of worth. *"And the LORD said unto Moses, Take thee Joshua the son of Nun, a man in whom is the spirit, and lay thine hand upon him; And set him before Eleazar the priest, and before all the congregation; and give him a charge in their sight."* (Numbers 27:18-19, KJV)

Moses placed Joshua before the priest and the entire congregation, putting him into a position of authority.

"My cup runneth over. Surely goodness and mercy shall follow me all the days of my life." (Psalm 23:5-6, KJV)

Finally, the shepherd should be GOOD to the sheep. The shepherd should show mercy. Mercy does not deal out what someone deserves.

An excellent way to break traditional cycles, generational cycles or even learned cycles is to remember mercy as opposed to always scolding the sheep or punishing them when they go astray.

Looking at one of the final phrases, "all the days of my life" reminds us parents should look beyond their child's 18th birthday or the time when the child leaves home. Employers should look beyond the last day the employee works. Pastors should look at what the individual may carry with them when they go somewhere else., regardless of their reason for leaving.

"And I will dwell in the house of the LORD forever." (Psalm 23:6, KJV)

The shepherd should provide a place one can call home. The parent should not say, "Well, if you leave now, you are never to come back again."

In Luke 15:11-32, we find the story of a selfish son who demanded his inheritance and left home. The son wasted his life and inheritance but was free to return home. The father waited and watched for his son's return.

The father saw him coming from a distance, and the waiting ended. He didn't keep waiting until the son traversed the final distance, fear growing by the second. Instead, the father ran to the son, greeted him, hugged him, and kissed him, welcoming the prodigal home. The father blessed him by putting a robe, a ring, and shoes upon him and celebrated his son's return. In fact, he threw a big party for him. As shepherds, we should do no less.

As children of The Good Shepherd, we look forward to that day when our Father welcomes us home. And at that moment, nothing we did or didn't do matters as He wraps His arms around us. But imagine the joy of going home obedient instead of approaching the end fearful because we remained in cycles instead of walking in God's grace and obedience to His will.

May it never be so.

Personal Evaluation

1. Who are your sheep and what are you willing to do to help them break the bondage of their cycle?

_____
_____
_____
_____
_____
_____
_____
_____

2. What kind of shepherd are you as a friend, caretaker, caregiver, leader, pastor or teacher?

_____
_____
_____
_____
_____
_____
_____
_____

3. What things might you do to become a better shepherd

4. What are some of the major things you are willing to make happen in your life to break chains off your life and the life of those you love and cherish?

5. Now that you have learned what it means to be in a "cycle" rather than being discouraged, despondent or disengaging, what are you willing to lose, lay aside or cast off so your load can become much lighter and you find it easier to follow Christ for yourself?

_____
_____
_____
_____
_____
_____
_____
_____

6. Because you recognize that living in true freedom is never going to be easy, what changes will you make sure so you continuously live in the liberty and freedom given to you at Calvary?

_____
_____
_____
_____
_____
_____
_____
_____

References

Donovan, R. N. (2009). *Biblical Commentary Deuteronomy 30:15-20*. Retrieved 07 08, 2019, from Sermon Writer Making Preaching More of a Joy: www.sermonwriter.com/biblical-commentary/deuteronomy-3015-20/

Everpedia International. (2019, 07 08). *Surrender (religion)*. Retrieved from Everpedia: www.everpedia.com

Fleming, V. (Director). (1939). *The Wizard of Oz* [Motion Picture].

White, E. G. (1943). *Counsels to Parents, Teachers and Students.* Pacific Pr Pub Assn; Reprint, Deluxe edition.

White, E. G. (1999). *Child Guidance.* Hagerstown, MD, USA: Review and Herald Publishing.

White, E. G. (2002). *Acts of the Apostles.* Pacific Press Publishing Assn.

White, E. G. (2009). *Christ's Object Lessons.* CreateSpace Independent Publishing Platform.

White, E. G. (2012). *An Appeal to Mothers.* A White Book .

White, E. G. (2013). *Our Father Cares.* Hagerstown, MD, USA: Review & Herald Publishing.

White, E. G. (2014). *The Paulson and Kress Collection of Ellen G. White Letters.* CreateSpace Independent Publishing Platform.

White, E. G. (2018). *Christian Temperance and Bible Hygiene.* CreateSpace Independent Publishing Platform.

Writeous Rhema. (2014, April 14). *Six of Satan's Devices of Which Not to be Ignorant.* Retrieved July 12, 2019, from writeousrhema.wordpress.come: www.writeousrhema.com

About the Author

Brenda Murphy is the Founder of Innovative Ministries, Inc., and the author and publisher of five books with several more in progress. Brenda writes from personal experiences and her daily walk with God.

Known for her spiritual wit, depth, and down-to-earth style, Brenda weaves colorful illustrations alongside biblical truth to help audiences find contentment, assuredness and endurance with the Lord. Through Brenda's signature wit and poignant story-telling, audiences are prompted to look beyond their circumstances and life situations to embrace, explore and receive the experiences of God's wonderful grace and mercy in the midst of adversity.

In her personal life and through her intimate walk with Christ, Brenda is discovering that every new day is a glorious fresh gift from God our heavenly Father to live in God-ordained purpose! Brenda truly believes that as sons and daughters of the Most High God, we can be confident, courageous and self-reliant in the fact that Jesus Christ, our Lord, loves us beyond our human comprehension. To prove it, we only need to read the Word of God for ourselves and believe in Him alone to find out just how much He really cares about everything that concerns us.

Brenda Murphy is a captivating and inspirational Christian author and popular conference speaker. She has conducted countless women's conferences and has been invited to speak extensively as a keynote speaker both locally and abroad.

Brenda has served as worship leader, intercessory prayer leader, Sunday school superintendent, counsellor, and life coach, as well as a host for family-life conferences, women's retreats, mother-and-daughter brunches, and single events.

Brenda uniquely weaves her life story and her powerful teaching to create a message of encouragement, hope, and motivation to all. A message that challenges everyone to keep their eyes focused on the real prize, and that is none other than Jesus Christ who is Lord over everything.

Brenda is happily married to the absolute love of her life, Audie, for more than 30 years, and she enjoys resting in the perfect will, purpose, and plan of God for their lives. Currently Brenda and Audie reside in the inspiring city of Fort Worth, Texas, which they proudly call home.

Other Books by Brenda Murphy

- *Had It Not Been For The Lord On Her Side*
- *Raw Faith*
- *Forgetting The Former Things*
- *Living In Purpose*

Coming Next:
- *Necessary Boundaries*
- *Spiritual Intruders*
- *Courage*

www.ingramcontent.com/pod-product-compliance
Lightning Source LLC
Chambersburg PA
CBHW060758110426
42739CB00033BA/3241